Are You Listening?

FOSTERING CONVERSATIONS THAT HELP YOUNG CHILDREN LEARN

Lisa Burman

Redleaf Press®
www.redleafpress.org
800-423-8309

Published by Redleaf Press
10 Yorkton Court
St. Paul, MN 55117
www.redleafpress.org

First edition 2009
Cover design by Jim Handrigan
Cover photographs by Steve Wewerka
Interior design by Mayfly Design
Typeset in Adobe Caslon Pro
Interior photographs provided by the author
Printed in the United States of America
21 20 19 18 17 16 15 14   6 7 8 9 10 11 12 13

Library of Congress Cataloging-in-Publication Data
Burman, Lisa, 1964-
    Are you listening? : Fostering conversations that help young children learn /
Lisa Burman.
        p. cm.
    Includes bibliographical references.
    ISBN 978-1-933653-46-4 (alk. paper)
    1. Children—Language. 2. Oral communication—Study and teaching
(Elementary). 3. Conversation—Study and teaching (Elementary) 4. Learning.
I. Title.
LB1139.L3B79 2008
372.1102'2—dc22
                              2007051927

Printed on acid-free paper

To the staff and students of PS 347, the American Sign Language and English Lower School, where I learned to listen with more than my ears.

ARE YOU LISTENING?

ACKNOWLEDGMENTS

As with many endeavors, this book is the result of the support and encouragement I have received from many people, and also the opportunities to work with committed and talented educators and wonderfully smart children. I would not have dreamed of writing a book by myself. The idea gradually emerged through the encouragement of two friends and colleagues in New York: Vicki Froomes (fellow education consultant) and Rebecca Marshall (principal of PS 347). Only after hearing "You should write" many, many times did I start to think it might be an idea worth trying. Thank you to Vicki and Rebecca for planting the seed of an idea and for believing I had a book within me.

I also wish to acknowledge and thank Diane and Greg Snowball, founders of A.U.S.S.I.E. (Australian United States Services in Education), for giving me the opportunity to work in New York City. Because of A.U.S.S.I.E. I began my work with the children and staff of PS 347, the American Sign Language and English Lower School, where I was able to explore and deepen my thinking about early childhood education.

My deepest gratitude and respect goes to the staff at PS 347. Your work with young learners provided me with the context for the thinking held within these pages. For collecting conversations and other documentation, for never tiring of talking with me about children's ideas, for your commitment to children and your own professional learning, and for your friendship, support, and encouragement—thank you!

Particular thanks to educators Susanne Harding, Sue Young, Vicki Froomes, Ellen Manobla, Marilla Baturay, Ned Brand, Peggy Lang, Dawn Slawitsky, Karen Giek, and Barbara Craft-Riess for your gentle and sincere reading of early drafts.

The way you thought with seriousness about the ideas in the writing and the feedback you gave instilled me with greater confidence in my writing.

To friends Susanne Harding, Sue Young, Kathryn Watson, Cathy O'Dea, Paul O'Dea, Leslie Tulloch, Max Greenwood, Lorraine Kennedy, Alan Wright, Colin Murray, Christine Murray, Bruce Williams, Helena Card, Tina Adamo, Ann Bliss, and Edgar Bliss who (just for the sheer fact of being fellow educators) had to endure endless conversations about children's conversations through lunches and dinner parties! Your generous listening and wisdom as educators allowed me to work through my thinking with trusted others.

Thank you to Leah Mermelstein for patiently answering all my "first-time writer" questions! Your experience with the process of writing for publication, your excitement, and your encouragement were incredibly helpful to this novice. Gratitude also to my Redleaf editors, Amanda Hane, for first believing in this project, and Beth Wallace, for patiently guiding me through the experience of writing a first book. Your feedback will help me continue to improve as a writer in the future.

I also wish to acknowledge the powerful work of the educators in Reggio Emilia, Italy. Their deep commitment to creating a future of hope through the education of young children remains a great inspiration and challenge to my work. While I did not intend *Are You Listening?* to be a "Reggio book" and I do not pretend in any way to be an expert on the depths of thinking and learning that occur there, there is no doubt my thinking and writing have been influenced by their ways of honoring the thinking of young learners. My gratitude to the educators of Reggio Emilia for sharing with the world, and my respect to them for continuing to push the boundaries of our imaginations.

A huge thank you to my family for supporting me in a million ways, all of which allow me to work on two continents and write a book in the midst of the madness. A sincere and special thank you to my sister, Michele, who supports my work and my life in so many ways. Your endless proofreading was incredibly valuable. Thank for enduring so much "teacher talk" during the writing process! Finally, I am deeply grateful to my parents, Ann and Len, for always believing I could achieve anything, and for encouraging me to do my best in whatever I chose to do, even writing a book! You helped me believe in myself enough to embark on such an unknown journey.

Introduction

"If we have two eyes, how come we only see one thing?"
—Anthony, 5 years

My young friend Anthony asked his mother the above question one weekend. Anthony is always asking questions. He continually surprises and delights us with his view of the world. Anthony's curiosity and inquisitiveness show his intelligence and potential for learning.

Unfortunately, at the time Anthony was wondering how the body works to help us see, his school experience was not supporting his curiosity. He had been in kindergarten for less than six months and his teacher had already warned his parents that he might need to repeat the year as he did not yet know his alphabet, his reading progress was limited, and he seemed disinterested in classroom activities.

The Problem of Disengaged Learners

The more I thought about it, the more Anthonys from my teaching experience came to mind. These are the children who think creatively, think divergently, and challenge teachers' ideas and beliefs. These are the children who continually ask Why? and scare teachers a little when they don't know the answer. These children are often not enriched or excited by their school experience. They're the children about whom teachers say, "I don't want her in my class next year" or "I don't know how you teach him, he'd drive me crazy!"

When Anthony's mother, Susan, first told me about her conversation with Anthony's teacher, I was angered by the failure of his school to value and tap into Anthony's intelligence and curiosity. I was worried that his teacher believed he was struggling with early literacy. I was surprised that she thought he needed to repeat kindergarten. However, I was most concerned about Anthony's disinterest in the learning opportunities provided for him at school. He was fast becoming a disengaged learner. I had known Anthony since he was a baby and this did not sound like the Anthony I knew. So what was wrong?

Anthony's teacher was focusing on a narrow definition of *effective learning*. Being a successful learner in Anthony's kindergarten class was defined by a limited set of skills and knowledge (knowing the alphabet, for example). While these skills play an important role in schooling, they are not the sole indicator of a successful learner.

Anthony had already shown he was very successful at learning. He was interested in understanding his world, and showed this by asking questions, being curious, and taking time to observe things and listen to others. One day, for example, he spent hours watching his pet guinea pigs adapt to their new environment, and told his family what he had noticed. He communicated well both with adults and his peers, and showed he could solve problems on his own when building a tower with blocks or negotiating with his siblings as they played in their playhouse. Anthony's school experience was not able to tap into his natural disposition toward learning, nor the skills he had developed during his early years. The problem was not with Anthony, but with the school.

Brittany is a different type of disengaged learner. She is quiet and complacent at school. She quietly participates in the learning experiences provided by her child care setting, often needing the encouragement of her teacher to join a new experience or to share what she is doing with the wider group. She tells me she is a "good girl" because she sits still and doesn't call out. She answers her teacher's questions only if she is confident her answer is what the teacher wants to hear, and doesn't easily take risks with new things at school. As she enters the classroom each morning, she holds tightly to her mother's hand and then sits quietly at the small table by the puzzles and waits for her teacher to come to her.

Brittany's mother is puzzled about her lack of excitement in school because at home she is constantly asking Why? about all kinds of things. She eagerly leads her younger sister to find worms in the garden, climbs trees at her grandparents' home, and carries her own notebook filled with drawings of people she knows. It seems Brittany has learned that school isn't about being excited and curious about the world, but is about pleasing the teacher and being a "good girl."

Initially, children such as Brittany seem like successful students. They rarely give teachers any trouble. However, scratch the surface and you find a passive learner, one whose potential is not tapped into. The Brittanys go through the motions and don't truly engage in learning. This type of learner is just as concerning as the disengaged learners who act out their frustration or disinterest, because the Brittanys are so often overlooked.

At four and five years of age, both Brittany and Anthony are already disengaging from the quest and joy of learning. If this continues, how will either child reach their full potential in future schooling and in life? How will their knowledge, skills, and dispositions for life-long learning fully develop? They are likely to miss opportunities to learn the intellectual skills needed for successful learning, such as setting goals, reflecting, evaluating, making plans, noticing details, solving problems, and asking questions. Literacy and mathematical skills need to be practiced in order to develop and consolidate. If Anthony and Brittany do not participate in school, they won't use their new skills and understandings, which will limit their growth and development. Our world is changing rapidly with new technologies and new challenges to sustainability. The one thing we can feel certain about in the future is that to be successful you will need to be flexible, be adaptable, and above all continue to learn. This is the world Anthony and Brittany are growing up in, so it is critical they become life-long learners.

Both these children are in danger of learning they are not good at learning. Brittany is in danger of seeing learning as something less than exciting and meaningful, and Anthony could very easily begin to believe he can't learn at all. A dangerous cycle of disengagement and possibly school failure could easily begin. Either child might eventually become so disinterested in school that they choose not to participate, and eventually drop out.

What is happening in early learning environments to cause young children to disengage with learning? Young children have a natural sense of wonder and curiosity about the world. Babies continually take in every new face that enters a room; toddlers are fascinated by the bubbles in their bathtub; four-year-olds want to know the reason for everything. What happens to this natural disposition and ability to be engaged in learning when children enter a more formalized early learning environment? What kind of curriculum leads to this disengagement?

The answer is simple: a curriculum, or a learning environment, that is planned without the child in mind. A curriculum that is designed by adults who, however well-meaning, have not spent enough time discovering each child's understanding of the world. A curriculum that is designed for a hypothetical group of learners cannot fully engage the diversity of emerging theories and possible confusions any group of particular learners will contain. "One size fits all" learning programs fail to consider the diversity of learning styles in a group of learners. Within a curriculum that narrows learning to one way of knowing, children like Anthony learn too quickly that they "cannot" learn, and children like Brittany limit their learning to comply with the curriculum. In fact, both children *can* learn. The curriculum, however, does not support them to think and learn in the way that most suits them; it doesn't engage them in the things that most interest and excite them. And so the Anthonys and Brittanys become disengaged, perhaps disruptive to others' learning or passive participants doing the bare minimum, because the curriculum is not planned with them in mind and doesn't help them answer *their* questions.

Conversations Engage Learners

While writing this book, I kept Anthony and Brittany in the back of my mind. So much more is possible for them. I want every child to feel the excitement and reward of learning something that is important and interesting to them. I want them to learn how to be successful, engaged, and self-directed learners who continue to learn because it enriches their lives. I dream of learning settings that show children how to be learners—forever. I want all children to believe they are smart and capable, to see they have contributions to make to the world. This dream must start with the youngest learners.

Engaging the Anthonys and Brittanys in their learning opportunities means planning curriculum with them in mind. There is no better way to do this than to engage them in conversations to discover what they already know, what they are curious about, and how they are beginning to understand their world. Valuing young learners' conversations and listening to children's ideas gives the Anthonys and Brittanys a voice in the classroom. Their ways of thinking and learning are valued and respected when teachers pay attention to conversations with them. Anthony is in a new classroom now where his teachers take his questions seriously and help him explore them. Because of this, Anthony continues to ask questions and is curious and inquisitive about the world. Brittany is at a new school where the teachers take time to get to know her ideas. Brittany now has the confidence to share *her* thoughts rather than go along with the crowd.

Both Anthony and Brittany feel more connected to, and therefore participate more in, all kinds of learning experiences in their new classrooms because there is a strong connection between their experience and their conversation. When they talk about their ideas, their vocabularies grow. When they listen to the ideas of others, their thinking is stretched. Participating in conversations gives them opportunities to practice and use skills in questioning, reflecting, planning, evaluating, and making connections, which are all essential skills for learning.

Most important, because the curriculum is now planned with them in mind, Anthony and Brittany understand that their ideas are important to the adults in their lives. This ensures that they develop a view of themselves as people who have positive contributions to make to the world around them.

Both kinds of learners, and all those in between, find more purpose in learning experiences that explore their own ideas about the world through conversations. In this kind of curriculum, children are engaged and excited about learning. They are motivated to search for answers to their questions and build understanding. They will develop dispositions and skills for learning—that is, they will be learning to learn. This will provide the firm foundation necessary for successful learning throughout school and throughout life.

Conversations Help Teachers

Teachers benefit from conversations that take place in the education setting too. Listening intently to young learners provides teachers with insight into children's understandings, ideas, and confusions. Instead of a "one size fits all" curriculum— which in reality does not fit many learners, particularly the Anthonys and Brittanys of the world—teachers will be able to use the knowledge gained through conversations with children to design the most engaging and challenging learning environment for them. Teachers will feel a closeness to the learners in their group—which empowers and energizes their work—and the excitement of learning along with them. When teachers commit to listening intently to young learners, they will be constantly surprised by their logic and intelligent thinking about the world.

Learning Environments Filled with Conversations

Many studies of the language used in educational settings have found that the teacher's voice is often the loudest in the room. Not necessarily the loudest in decibels, but the majority of the talking in many education settings is done by adults, not children. In learning environments where teachers do most of the talking, conversations often have characteristics such as:

- teachers control the conversation with question-and-answer drills
- conversations flow only from teacher to child and back again
- questions lead the conversation to one way of thinking about the topic, or to one "right" answer

- teachers mentally mark children's ideas as "right" or "wrong"
- teachers control all aspects of the learning experience by only giving directions and instructions to young learners (this is called "one-way talk")
- teachers ignore children's ideas because they don't understand them
- teachers do not give children enough time to think and fully explain their ideas before moving on
- conversations are rushed to fit into tightly planned schedules or the teacher's own agenda

In this situation, how can teachers learn how children see and understand the world? How do children come to believe their ideas are important to the adults in their lives? Where is the opportunity for children to ask questions that are important to them, or to explore their own thinking? In this kind of environment, children learn that only adult thinking is important. The balance needs to change. We need to hear children's voices more clearly in early learning settings.

What does it look like when conversations in learning environments serve to explore children's thinking and deepen their learning? In these environments, conversations have characteristics such as:

- learners' voices are heard the most
- teacher talk seeks to discover children's ideas
- children talk with each other
- children have time to think
- topics connect to children's interests, explorations, and questions
- conversations are documented and interpreted to reveal thinking
- conversation is used to stretch children's thinking

How do teachers make this happen? It takes more than just sitting down to listen to children—although that's a good start! The program culture must support conversations among children and between children and teachers in a variety of ways. In an early learning environment with a strong culture of conversation, teachers do these things:

- provide time and space for conversations throughout the day
- encourage conversations between young learners as well as conversations between teachers and children
- show a genuine interest in discovering children's thinking and ideas by listening intently to them
- believe young learners are capable of intelligent and abstract thinking about topics that are important to them, and take children's comments

seriously, asking for more information or clarification if they don't understand

- provide active and authentic experiences that give young learners something worthwhile and meaningful to talk about
- document conversations and use them to reveal learning, connect with families, develop children's learning dispositions and skills, and guide curriculum planning
- work collaboratively with one another and with children's families, seeking to learn more about the ideas children's conversations reveal

This book is about creating a culture of conversation in early childhood programs. This book will show you how to listen more and talk less, and how to focus the conversations in your learning environment on children's real interests. You'll learn how to set up your environment to promote children's conversations, and how to facilitate large and small group conversations. And finally, this book will help you document and interpret what you hear so that you can construct curriculum to engage the children in your environment.

Learning from Other Teachers' Stories

I have been an early childhood educator for many years now. I began my teaching career in a small rural school in Australia. I currently serve as an education consultant in Australia and the United States. Over the past six years or so I have been thinking more deeply about how we can more fully engage all children in learning opportunities. I believe that teachers need to listen more intently to children's thinking and to explore the potential of conversations to do so.

While the seeds to my thinking were sown many years ago during my efforts to build a collaborative and democratic classroom, it was my study tour to Reggio Emilia in northern Italy that transformed my wonderings about children's thinking into a passion. During the opening address in Reggio Emilia, within the first five minutes, I felt I had come home professionally. I was soon jolted out of my easy comfort when I realized that the depth of thinking about children's learning in Reggio Emilia was actually the greatest challenge for me. The Reggio educators challenged me to deepen my thinking about curriculum design, and energized me to continue the journey of creating a different kind of schooling experience for young learners.

Through my role as a consultant, I have been given the incredible opportunity to work and learn with many talented educators. *Are You Listening?* shares with you the ways some of these teachers have responded to the challenge of listening intently to young learners during our professional learning work together. The words on the pages come to life through the stories of staff members and students from PS 347, the American Sign Language and English Lower School in Manhattan (which has a long and proud history since when it was known as J47). I have worked intensively with this community since 2002, often consulting weekly with them. My responsibility as a consultant is to facilitate the professional learning of teachers. Through this work, the teachers and I have been exploring the meaning behind children's words and how conversations can be used to reveal their thinking. The PS 347 teachers question and experiment with different ways of listening deeply to children's ideas. They learn together, they learn from their mistakes, and most of all they continue to learn from the children they work with.

PS 347 is situated on a busy Manhattan street. It is an elementary school from prekindergarten to sixth grade, with six prekindergarten classes. In a dual-language program, children are taught about and taught in the languages of American Sign Language and English. To provide strong language models for the children, each class has two teachers: one who is a first-language American Sign Language user, and the other a first-language English user. The students include children who are Deaf, hard of hearing, and hearing. Many of the hearing students have a Deaf relative, quite often one or both parents. Therefore, the first language of these children is American Sign Language. Many early childhood settings include children whose first language is other than the primary language of a society. Your context may be different from this, but the common human experiences of communicating, being in a relationship, and learning together will bind us together as you read.

The ideas in *Are You Listening?* have been lived. They have been tried and tested in real learning situations. Other stories come from home environments, from child care settings, and from some of my young friends (I've changed their names to fictional ones). As you read, you will meet learners who are young and not so young. They have all enriched my understanding of learning and teaching, and I hope their stories do the same for you.

How to Use *Are You Listening?*

Are You Listening? begins with a discussion of learning theory. Chapter 1 discusses theories of learning and the ways in which conversation helps children learn. It also helps you explore your view of children and the ways in which this contributes to your work with children.

Chapter 2 looks at the characteristics and types of conversations that engage children's minds and support their learning.

Ensuring that young learners have a voice in their learning environment does not happen by chance; it takes forethought and planning. Chapter 3 discusses implications for the learning environment and curriculum design. I share practical suggestions for room arrangement, scheduling, organization of materials, and the most effective learning experiences for nurturing conversation.

The role of the teacher in facilitating conversations is explored in chapter 4. Through examples and stories from various learning environments, we'll talk about strategies for grouping learners, asking questions, delving deeper to search for children's understandings, and managing conversations.

Teachers need systems and strategies to support them in listening to children's ideas. Chapter 5 details structures and strategies you can use to capture children's voices for use in interpretation and planning. The nuts and bolts of how to collect conversations and how to decide which conversations are worth collecting and transcribing are included. You will also find suggestions for getting started by setting realistic and manageable goals for yourself.

This sets the scene for the next chapter, where the process of documentation is taken further. Chapter 6 shares strategies for interpreting conversations and building understandings of the emerging theories of young learners. It advocates for interpreting conversations within a collaborative process. Ways to create a culture of conversation with your colleagues and children's families are also discussed.

This book is about conversations. But what about the children in your setting who do not participate in conversations, for whatever reason? Perhaps they have a "language delay" or developing speech. Perhaps their first language is different from the primary learning language in your setting and they are frustrated in their efforts to express themselves. How can you listen to them? How can you empower their voices to be heard in your learning setting? Chapter 7 discusses the challenge of listening to a child with developing language. I use examples of real children and their teachers to explain how teachers listened to the children's drawing, play, and construction and valued their thinking as it was expressed in ways other than speech.

Finally, you will want to use the understanding and knowledge you gain from facilitating, collecting, and interpreting conversations. Your insights can be used to engage children in learning and enrich their experience. Chapter 8 discusses ways to use conversations to communicate with families, to share with children (which helps develop learning skills such as self-reflection and goal setting), and to guide your curriculum planning. Examples of ways to stretch the thinking of young learners through their play, drawing, construction, exploration with materials, field trips, and further conversations connect learning theory to your daily learning and teaching practice.

Pedagogical conversations are critical to ensure your learning process continues after you finish reading this book. It is not only more difficult but more limiting to try new ideas in isolation. By engaging in conversation with your colleagues, you will hear alternative perspectives that can stretch your own understanding. Just as we acknowledge the importance of children learning from conversations with each other, you will benefit as a teacher from learning in conversation with your colleagues. It offers you the opportunity to develop new insights into your relationships with children and their families and your role in facilitating learning. Your ideas and theories about learning and about teaching practice (and those of your colleagues) can be challenged, confronted, affirmed, and enriched. Throughout *Are You Listening?* you will find sections called "Taking Ownership." These activities are included in the hope you will meet with your colleagues to discuss your reading, and use the "Taking Ownership" suggestions to guide your thinking and make your reading relevant to your own context. There is a saying "Many hands make light work," to which I add "Many minds make rich learning."

Two aspects of my writing to note before reading: you will notice I chose to alternate the gender-specific language in chapters. I did so to support the clarity of reading, not to make any statement about gender roles in education. I use the terms "teacher," "educational setting," "learning environment," and "family" inclusively. That is, the term "teacher" is used to describe all adults working with young learners in an educational setting. In my mind, this includes university-qualified teachers, teaching assistants, home-based child care providers, and other professionals such as speech teachers, social workers, and occupational therapists who may be working with children in learning settings. I have used the term "educational setting" or "learning environment" to include primary and elementary schools; prekindergarten programs within schools; private, community, and church-based prekindergarten or early learning centers; and home-based child care programs. Rather than use the term "parent," I have chosen to use "family" in an effort to include nontraditional forms of family such as grandparents, extended families, foster parents, and other guardians.

The most talented educators I have worked with are those who view theory and research as a tool by which to view the world, children, and the learning environment. Theory isn't just read about and discussed, but becomes a living reality as teachers connect it to the learning that happens in their setting. They use theory and research not as an end, but as a stepping-off point for developing their own theories and beliefs about learning. They learn from other educators but always reflect on their own context and make decisions that fit with the unique lives and interests of their setting, their teaching, and their young learners. It is my hope that during the reading of this book, you will develop and deepen your own personal theories about the relationship between learning and teaching. *Are You Listening?* is my invitation to you to take ownership of the ideas you read and think about, and to integrate them with your own prior knowledge and experience, transforming them as you need and making them your own. In doing so you begin the challenging journey of reaching children like Anthony and Brittany who need, above all, someone to be interested enough to truly listen to them.

CHAPTER ONE

Learning and Your View of the Child

It is important for teachers to understand learning theory. A theory of learning seeks to explain how learning happens. It is a set of beliefs about learning, and subsequently about teaching. When you read and think about theory, you form your own set of beliefs about learning. It is this set of beliefs, or personal theories, that guide your daily actions and words as a teacher. In turn, your actions and words create conditions that either support conversations for learning, or stifle opportunities for children to talk and listen to each other. If you want to build a culture of conversation to engage young learners, it is essential to understand the theories that explain how children learn through conversation.

Another reason it is important to develop a clear personal theory is because theory forms a lens through which you view the world. Experiences, observations, and conversations are interpreted by individuals through their own lens of beliefs and values.

For example, several teachers might see the same child throw a block but have very different ideas about the child's motivation for doing so. One teacher might think the child is being naughty. Another teacher might say the child is trying to get attention. Yet another teacher might say the child is showing her frustration at not having the vocabulary to explain what she wants. Each of these views is the result of that person's theories about learning and about children. The first teacher believes, perhaps unconsciously, that children are bad until they're taught to be good. The second teacher believes that children constantly seek attention, and so behave in ways to get it. The third teacher believes that children's behavior can be an outward sign of their inner feelings.

The best way to bring clarity to your personal learning theory is to read and talk with your colleagues about theories from researchers and other writers. These theories will inform, challenge, and develop your own theories: the theories through which you view children's learning.

For theory to make sense to you it needs to connect to your context—to your daily work with young learners. In order to develop and enrich your personal theories of learning, you need to understand how these theories work in practice. It is not enough to be able to verbalize a list of learning beliefs. Teachers must be able to talk about what children are doing and how this relates to learning theory. Otherwise, theory remains words on a page. It is your lived experience—your daily learning and teaching practices—that give the words life and meaning. When you connect theory to practice, you will have more of those "a-ha" moments of clarity and understanding. You can connect theory to your context by asking questions such as:

- Where do I see children learning the way this theory says they do?
- What have I experienced with children that agrees or disagrees with this theory?
- Does this theory make sense in terms of the way I learn most effectively?
- Does this theory make sense with the other things I believe about learning?
- Does this theory challenge me to think differently about learning?

So often teachers use theory or research to prove they are on the "right" path or teaching the "right" way. There isn't one right way to teach all learners—in fact, it is very dangerous to promote such an idea. Promoting one right way of teaching can stop teachers from thinking about the real children in their program when designing curriculum, and takes them away from planning with those children in mind. Instead, teachers follow a recipe for the perfect lesson plan, the perfect environment, the "one right way" to teach. When teachers follow someone else's idea of what is right for children (which so often takes the form of a packaged curriculum), they stop following the children. In this book I promote an alternative way of designing curriculum, one that allows teachers to follow the learner rather than follow the book. You can do this by creating a culture of conversation in your learning setting and facilitating conversations that engage children in thinking and learning. The spotlight is back on the learning, highlighting the wondrous and unpredictable dance that happens between the learner and the learning process.

Theory is essential to teachers' growth as educators. The most important consideration is how you *use* theory and research. Are you using theory to prove you are doing the "right" thing, or are you using it to deepen and challenge your thinking? It is more powerful for your learning, and subsequently for the learning of the children, to use theory to deepen and challenge your own personal theories. This chapter will present some theory about how young children learn and the role conversation plays in facilitating this learning. This will lay a foundation upon which to build your own personal theories about learning and teaching.

How Do Children Learn?

First, I would like to define what I mean when I use the word "learning." Throughout the world, in many different early learning environments, there are many different ideas of what learning is, but these ideas are rarely defined clearly by those working closely with young learners. A traditional, but common, view sees learning as the ability to copy what the teacher does. For example, if Anthony can sing the alphabet song the way the teacher showed him, it means he has learned the alphabet. If he can make a rabbit like the teacher's model with perfectly shaped ears, a nose, and three whiskers on each side, it means he knows the features and characteristics of a rabbit. If Brittany can tell the teacher the right answer to the question, it means she has learned the information. This view of learning is concerned with covering the curriculum set by the teacher—the kind of curriculum that is designed *without* the child in mind.

However, many teachers and theorists hold a very different view of learning. This definition of learning is concerned with *understanding*, not mere replication or regurgitation of facts. From this perspective, copying a behavior or recalling a list of facts does not show that Anthony and Brittany are engaged in learning. Perhaps Anthony already recognizes many letters of the alphabet, but is made to sit through many lessons of reciting the alphabet anyway and doesn't learn anything new. Perhaps Brittany is confused about how water becomes ice and steam, but because she answers the teacher's questions with the "right" answers this is never discovered. Teachers whose theory includes an active learning perspective look, for example, to see that Anthony has built some understanding about the alphabetic principle, how letters are grouped together to form words, and how these communicate a message when he writes a list of items he needs to pack for a ski vacation in the mountains. Teachers who want to see that Brittany understands something about the transformative properties of water will observe and talk with her about her knowledge when she makes Jell-O or watches a teakettle boil. These experiences tell teachers that children have developed an understanding—or have *learned*—more clearly than imitating what the teacher did and giving the "right" answers to closed questions will.

Are You Listening? was written using certain beliefs about how children most effectively learn. Understanding these ideas will help you connect them with your own context and your own theory of learning. The following ideas are essential for understanding the value of conversation in engaging young learners:

- Learners actively construct their own understandings.
- Learning begins with prior knowledge.
- Learning takes place in authentic and social contexts.
- Conflict is essential to learning.

Learners Actively Construct Their Own Understanding

Many theorists agree that learning is an active process (Garhart Mooney 2000). Learning is not a one-way street of obtaining knowledge or being filled up the way an empty jug is filled with water. It is a much more complex and dynamic process wherein each learner is *active* in making sense of new information or new experiences. Recent brain research supports the belief that learners actively construct their own understanding through experience (Jensen 2005). Learners are most likely to remember and understand what they learn if they are challenged to make the connections themselves. Young children in particular need to be active participants in the learning process. Instead of being told a person's shadow will follow them as they move, for example, it is more effective for a young learner to discover this as she watches her friend's shadow move around the playground with her, or as she makes shadow puppets with her hands. She will understand that her shadow moves with her because she has actively experienced it, and therefore has actively constructed her learning. This theory challenges teachers to reflect on how early learning environments can be active places where young learners are themselves directly involved in exploring, thinking, talking, questioning, and connecting ideas.

Learning Begins with Prior Knowledge

Every learner comes to a learning situation with an already-established worldview. For example, take a look at this conversation about snow a teacher had with two four-year-olds:

Teacher:	Look out the window! What can you see?
Manny:	It's snowing!
Eve:	Snow come down!
Teacher:	What happens when it snows?
Eve:	Put boots on.
Manny:	And my coat. I built a snowman with my dad and we put a carrot on.
Eve:	And my scarf for snowman.
Teacher:	Your snowman had a scarf? What else happened when you were in the snow?
Manny:	And I throwed a snowball at Dad!
Teacher:	Oh, no! What happened?
Manny:	He got me and in the snow and we had to put our boots outside.

Manny and Eve have a wealth of knowledge about snow. Their prior knowledge has been learned through their life experiences. This worldview or prior knowledge is sometimes referred to as *schema* (Owocki 1999, 42). With new experiences and interactions, this schema evolves, develops, and changes. When the learner connects a new experience or idea to an existing schema, learning occurs. This is the active process of constructing understanding. Your role as the teacher is to provide experiences that challenge young learners' thinking so new connections can be made. To do this effectively you need to know as much as you can about the children's prior knowledge. By first discovering the children's prior knowledge and experience, you can identify the best kind of learning experience to provide next. Without knowledge of the children's prior knowledge, you might provide an experience that does not challenge the children's schema or that is too far removed from their prior knowledge to make connections and integrate the new experience with their existing schema.

Taking Ownership

Brainstorm a list of what you believe is the prior knowledge of the children in your group. What experiences and understanding do they bring with them when they enter your class or center? What prior knowledge and experience may be unique to a particular child or a group of children?

How can you honor, value, and utilize the particular prior knowledge and experience of different cultural groups of the families in your class, school, or center?

Learning Takes Place in Authentic and Social Contexts

Learning does not happen in an isolation room in our brain. Learning is connected to our experience of the world, which gives it meaning for the learner. According to Montessori and Piaget, the most engaging learning experiences are connected to the context of the child's real-life experience (Garhart Mooney 2000). Learning about the life cycles of plants is more meaningful and engaging when learned while planting and growing sunflowers than by coloring pictures of seeds, sun, water, leaves, and flowers. Growing sunflowers is an authentic context for learning.

Manny and Eve's conversation about snow was connected to something very real to them because they had real-life experience with snow. They brought their prior knowledge to the conversation, and because it concerned their immediate experience, they had something to say about it. Learning connected to experiences and ideas relevant to children's lives are more likely to draw them into participation. Using these relevant topics also ensures that children have some experience or ideas to bring to the conversation. Their participation will be much richer. They will engage with the experience and their learning because it is real to them.

Learners also construct understanding through social interaction. Vygotsky (1978) regarded the role of social interaction as the most powerful experience for facilitating learning. When children talk and listen to one another, they have the opportunity to encounter differing ideas and theories about the world. These new ways of understanding can provide the stimulus for constructing new learning. The context provides a shared experience to talk about and explore. When young learners interact with friends and with adults, their ideas are stretched and their understanding is deepened.

For example, imagine Josh, Carlos, and Kelli-Ann, all four years old, working together to build a spaceship with cardboard boxes. Through their interactions with each other they learn different ways to solve problems and construct with boxes, and also new ideas about spaceships. Josh shows his friends how to cut a box so it stands flat. Carlos tells the other children exciting stories about the spaceship's flight to space and engages them in imagining what their spaceship will be able to do. When Kelli-Ann insists the top of the spaceship needs to be pointy and shows the boys a photo from a book on space travel to explain exactly what she means, their schema is stretched and new understandings are constructed.

Conflict Is Essential to Learning

In many societies, conflict is often thought about in terms of social conflict, and as a problem to be avoided. However, intellectual conflict is a necessary requirement for learning. There needs to be something that conflicts with a learner's existing schema to shake up thinking. Without an unfamiliar experience, an alternative perspective, new information, or a different idea for the learner to connect to her existing schema or prior knowledge, there is no shift in understanding.

Intellectual conflict can happen between two or more people with different ideas or theories, like when Kelli-Ann showed Josh and Carlos that it was important for the spaceship to have a pointy top. This was a source of intellectual conflict for Josh and Carlos.

Conflict also occurs within the thinking of individual learners when an experience challenges their existing schema. Collecting snowballs and observing how they change when brought indoors could be an experience of intellectual conflict for Manny and Eve and challenge them to construct new understandings about the properties of snow.

Think of two-year-old Sam for a moment. Through his play with tennis balls, beach balls, and basketballs, he has developed the schema that balls bounce. When he is given a beanbag ball, he expects it to act the same as a tennis ball, because his schema tells him that balls bounce. However, when Sam throws the beanbag ball to the ground, expecting it to bounce back toward him, it doesn't. The new experience with the beanbag ball is a source of conflict with Sam's existing ideas about balls, and leads him to modify his schema. The educators in Reggio Emilia often refer to this intellectual conflict as a *provocation* (Edwards, Gandini, and Forman 1998). In chapter 2 of *Are You Listening?* we will explore ways facilitated conversation can provide the opportunity for such intellectual conflict.

Taking Ownership

What do you believe about learning? Make a list of how you believe young children learn best. Don't refer to any books or curriculum documents, just write from your heart and from your head. It is important to be in touch with your own beliefs as a teacher.

How do your actions as a teacher display these beliefs? Grab a notebook and write down each belief statement as a heading on a separate page. Underneath each heading, write all the ways you show this belief about learning in your daily teaching. How do your actions, the materials you provide, the language you use with children, the daily schedule, and your interactions with families show your beliefs? Do you notice any mismatch between what you say you believe and what you do each day?

Why Is Conversation Important to Learning?

Given the understanding that learning most effectively occurs within a social context, the role that conversation plays in facilitating learning becomes clear. Conversation is the most powerful tool for communicating our understanding, ideas, feelings, and confusions with each other. It engages children in the process of actively constructing their understanding of the world because:

- Talk organizes thinking.
- Language reveals prior knowledge.
- Conversations provide a context for social learning.

Talk Organizes Thinking

Talk, whether internalized self-talk or externalized conversation, is one of our most powerful tools for organizing our thinking (Ritchhart 2002). By the time I discovered this about myself as a learner, it was too late to have any positive impact on my high-school education. Throughout my years of schooling I was a lot like Brittany. I was a successful student but I learned to pass tests and get good grades because I wanted to please my family and my teachers. I wasn't engaged in learning because I didn't always see the relevance or have an investment in understanding what was being taught. I was focused on passing tests and getting good grades, not on understanding things. I didn't realize the power of talking to help me understand, and so now I remember very little about many things I learned in high-school mathematics, history, science, and geography. I read and studied novels in English class, but I cannot talk to you about them now. I rarely spoke in class because I was afraid I would say the wrong answer to the teacher's question, or would be seen as stupid because I didn't understand something. So I did not tap into the powerful tool of talk in order to understand and subsequently remember this new knowledge.

In his illuminating book *Seeing Voices*, Oliver Sacks talks of the absolute need human beings have for language. He shows how poor communication "leads not only to intellectual constriction but to timidity and passivity," and how a culture that provides many opportunities for rich conversation "awakens the imagination and mind, leads to a self-sufficiency, a boldness, a playfulness, a humor, that will be with the person for the rest of his life" (55).

We require language to become thinkers. Sacks says, "We start with dialogue, with language that is external and social, but then to think, to become ourselves, we have to move to a monologue, to inner speech" (59). Our internal talk is our thinking in action. It is where our thinking takes place. Our thinking is dependent on our inner language, our ability to speak to ourselves—and because of this, our thinking and our continued development as cognitive beings *also* is dependent upon *external* conversation. It is through conversation with others that we learn how to use language to begin with. Put simply, we learn language by talking, and then we can talk to ourselves about our ideas. Conversation is the universal shared language of learning.

Taking Ownership

Take a moment to think about the children in your setting and the ways they are currently learning. What are you curious about? Are you wondering about their social learning in the imaginative play area? Are you curious about the kinds of learning happening in the sand play? Do the interactions at the painting easel intrigue you? Whatever it is, spend ten minutes journaling about it. Don't worry about the grammar, spelling, or style of writing; just put your thoughts on paper. After you have done this, step back from the writing for a moment. What happened to your ideas as you put them into words? How did your language help you to organize your thinking?

Language Reveals Prior Knowledge

Children's talk reveals glimpses of their prior knowledge about the world. Recognizing these glimpses will help you create engaging learning experiences for them. Remember Manny and Eve's conversation about snow? Their language revealed part of their prior knowledge and experience of snow. It showed that they understood:

- how snow felt
- that snow could be manipulated to stay together in different shapes when building snowmen
- that snow was cold, and when it snowed it meant the weather was also cold
- that you needed to wear certain clothes when you went out in the snow
- that you could have fun with your family in the snow
- that boots you had worn in the snow didn't belong inside

By understanding the importance of children's prior knowledge, you know where to start when building a curriculum. For example, the starting place for learning about snow would be very different for children in Hawaii who had never seen snow than for Manny and Eve who have different prior knowledge. These two groups of learners will need to begin with different experiences in order to create intellectual conflict and stretch their schema. Listening carefully to children's conversations will give you the information you need to design the most engaging learning experiences for your unique group of young learners.

Conversations Provide a Context for Social Learning

You provide many social learning opportunities in your educational setting, such as block construction and imaginative play. Within these opportunities, conversations between the children provide a context for learning: children listen to other ideas or perspectives, and they discuss, negotiate, and build on one another's ideas. Your facilitation will guide conversations to ensure that children listen to one another and make connections between new ideas. Without children talking about their experiences and their thinking, this active connection-making is left to chance. Conversation is social by its very nature, and provides young learners with the place, time, and challenge to share their experiences, thinking, and questions. Notice the rich exchange of ideas in the conversation I had with six-year-olds Nicholas and Charlie about how they learned to whistle. Their thinking seems to feed off each other's ideas.

Lisa (adult): How did you learn to whistle?

Nicholas: I didn't really *learn* to whistle.

Lisa:	But you can whistle now, can't you? How did it happen?
Nicholas:	No one actually *taught* me how to whistle.
Lisa:	That's interesting. So you didn't need someone else to teach you to whistle?
Charlie:	You can just look in books and study and stuff.
Lisa:	So did you do that to learn to whistle, Nick?
Nicholas:	No [laughing]. Not whistling! One day it just slipped out.
Charlie:	I learned to whistle when I was doing something with this toy plane and then went . . . [makes whistling sound and shows how his arm carried the toy plane like it was flying]
Nicholas:	Actually, I was at school and one of my friends was whistling and I tried it and I could do it. I looked at him and I could do it!
Charlie:	You just have to learn and try, that's all.

Learning and Teachers' Views of Children

The five-year-olds in Peggy and Dave's kindergarten class have been exploring and creating the most wondrous structures with blocks. At the end of each Investigation Time, the teachers ask the children to decide to either pack away the blocks or leave them up so they can continue with the work the following day. Felicity, Karin, and Annie have been creating a snowflake factory with the blocks for almost two weeks. They elaborate on the design each day, and have written small signs that inform visitors about its different areas. They have made adults and children out of cardboard and Popsicle sticks and placed them throughout the factory. The girls have created stories about the snowflake factory and the activities the cardboard people undertake within its walls.

As I enter the classroom this particular Wednesday, Peggy calls me over and tells me about a dilemma that has arisen. "It's not fair," Bryce, a student, tells Peggy. "They do the blocks every day." "We want a turn," Edward, another student, joins in. "I think they have a legitimate point, but I'm not sure the best way to handle it and respect the work of all the children. I think Dave and I need to talk about it before we decide just to ask the girls to pack it away," explains Peggy.

The way that Peggy and Dave decide to proceed with this very natural and regular classroom dilemma will speak volumes about the way they view the children in their care, and childhood generally. If they decide to direct Felicity, Karin, and Annie to pack away the snowflake factory so Bryce and Edward can play with the

The snowflake factory

blocks, the teachers are taking control of the situation. This decision reflects the idea that children are incapable of negotiating, problem solving, or making a just decision so the teacher needs to do it for them.

An alternative view of childhood, however, is one where children are in fact capable of thinking and decision making. If Peggy and Dave hold this alternative idea of children, they will trust them to make a decision about the blocks and will relinquish control to them while guiding the process. After Peggy and Dave discuss the situation, this is what they decide to do. Once given time to reflect on their beliefs about children, they see no other possible way but to ask the children, "How do you think we could work it out?"

I return to the kindergarten class the following morning to discover Peggy, Dave, and the children sitting in a semicircle facing the snowflake factory. They are holding a class meeting and the children are deciding how to negotiate a solution to their problem. The girls have explained their work, and it is evident how hard they have worked on the factory. Bryce and Edward talk about how they feel left out and their desire to play with the blocks too. The teachers guide the children to make a list of possible solutions, which are written on a chart. They return to the discussion later that day, and the children decide together that the girls will have two more days to work on their snowflake factory. During these two days, they will decide how they want to capture the experience so it can be remembered after it is packed away at the end of Friday's Investigation Time. The boys (and anyone else who wants to) can begin their block play on Monday. The children make this decision themselves, with the guidance of their teachers to ensure that they considered different options and that everyone's view was heard. Felicity, Karin, and Annie work solidly on Thursday and Friday to create representations of their snowflake factory: taking photographs for a book they would continue making the following week, drawing a floor plan on a large sheet of paper, and writing part of their snowflake story. They feel completely comfortable when Friday afternoon comes and it is time to pack away their elaborate work.

This story illustrates how important it is to be aware of our own view about childhood, as it informs all our decision making as educators. Your ideas about children will influence how you create conversational moments and how you interact with young learners during these conversations.

Your View of Children as Learners

Just like Dave and Peggy, it is important for you to have a clear idea about how you view children. What do you think about children? What do you believe about children as learners and as people in relationship with you? Adults tend to hold a view of children as either empty or competent. Whichever view you hold (or wherever you fit in between the two extremes), it influences how you treat children: how you interact with them, how you question them, and how you respond to their ideas and emerging theories about the world. As you read about two views of children in the next section, consider what you believe about children and what you see in the children you work with.

THE EMPTY CHILD

Teachers who view children as empty see:

- children as blank slates: empty, ready to be filled up with knowledge
- children as not capable of making decisions, solving problems, or negotiating independently; children as needing an adult to make decisions for them
- children as developmentally immature and not ready for more complex or abstract thinking and hypothesizing
- children as isolated, individual learners

- children as dependent on the more competent adult to learn
- learning happening when the teacher directs the experience and children follow what the teacher wants them to do
- prior knowledge and experience (the learning that happens before and outside of school) as unimportant. In fact, for some, the empty child does not have *any* prior knowledge that is useful or relevant to school learning
- a need for the curriculum to start at the same place and follow the same path for all children

If Dave and Peggy held this view, the children in their class would not have been trusted to make a decision about the snowflake factory because the teachers would have believed they were not capable of such thinking and problem solving. Teachers who hold the empty-child viewpoint might have solved the dilemma by telling the girls they had played with the blocks long enough and had to pack them away to let other children have a turn. Their rationale for this action might have been that the girls are "just too young" to negotiate and see another's perspective or are not developmentally ready for this step. In this view, children need the more competent adults to make the decision for them because they can't do it for themselves.

It may seem extreme to discuss the empty-child view this way. How could anyone who has ever met a child think of him or her as empty? And yet, if you pay attention, you will see how much curriculum is predicated on the belief that children are not competent and do not have any important prior knowledge.

THE COMPETENT CHILD

Teachers who hold the competent-child view see:

- children as knowledgeable and capable
- children as independent learners, not solely dependent on an adult for all learning
- children as resourceful: they have strategies and skills they can use to learn, invent, communicate, think, problem solve, and create
- children as social beings, learning from their relationships with others (both adults and other children)
- learning can and does happen when the teacher is not directly there with the children
- prior knowledge and learning from outside the school experience as important and valued in the same way as the learning that happens in school

- curriculum as open and fluid to respond to the many different pathways of learning and multiple ways children make meaning of the world; that is, it is not a "one size fits all" program

The competent-child viewpoint aligns with the learning theory we explored earlier. If you believe learning is actively constructed by the learner, it follows that you see children as *capable* of constructing this knowledge. Otherwise your personal theory about learning and your view of children don't match.

When you believe children are capable of complex and abstract thinking, you see their ideas and emerging theories as the way they make sense of the world, and value them as such. If you instead regard these emerging ideas as wrong or just cute you devalue children's thinking and do not see how they are competent in connecting ideas with their schema.

If you believe learning begins with prior knowledge and that all learners have their own unique schema about how the world works, you must also view children as competent, because they come to you with existing ideas and experiences to build on. You cannot view children as blank slates because their prior learning and understanding are part of them already.

When you believe conflict is essential to learning, you must also see children as capable of learning from conflict. That is, you see children as able to independently construct new understandings when faced with a provocation or an experience that shakes up their thinking.

When you believe the most effective learning takes place within social and authentic contexts, you see children as capable of learning from others (both adults and other children). You believe that a child can be both a learner and a teacher in this social learning context. If you believe learning only happens when the teacher is present, that is, that learning is dependent on the more competent adult, then your view of children does not match your belief in the social aspect of learning.

Take a moment to imagine visiting an early learning setting where the teacher views children as competent. What do you see and hear? You hear conversations between children, not just from teacher to child, because the teacher understands how children are capable of learning from each other. The teacher is crouching down or sitting at the same level as the children, looking intently into their faces as they talk, showing his interest in the children's ideas. He values these conversations for their insight into the thinking and ideas of the young learners. You see this by the way the teacher does not interrupt the child who is talking, and asks questions to clarify and ensure he understands what the child means to communicate. The teacher takes the children's ideas seriously; he shows this by actively listening and frequently writing down the children's words. Because the teacher views the children as smart, capable, resourceful, and knowledgeable, he is very interested in what each child has to say. You could even say the teacher is *fascinated* by the children's view of the world. This is one of the largest differences between the two views of children: the adult who sees children as competent is interested in *listening to* them; the adult who sees children as empty just wants to talk to them.

If teachers see children as competent, why do their actions and words not always match this view? Why do teachers struggle with living out this competent view in their daily interactions with young learners? Often they continue teaching in ways that are so embedded in their subconscious that they are unaware of the reasons they act that way. Teaching involves many decisions each day and it is very easy (and often efficient) to make quick decisions or to continue with old habits without considering which view of children is being reflected. When deciding if your words and actions reflect a competent view of children or not, it is helpful to reflect on why you do certain things. Maybe it's for one of these reasons:

- I've always done it this way.
- That's the way it was done when I came to the center/school.
- I learned to do it this way when I was at college.
- It's easier if I do it this way.
- The other teachers do it, and they've been teaching longer than me.
- It's quicker if I do it than if I let the children do it.
- The children can't do it on their own.

The snowflake-factory story from earlier in this chapter shows how important it was for Peggy and Dave to stop and think before they made a quick decision on what to do about the situation. Now that they have successfully experienced handing over the decision making to the children, they will continue to look for further opportunities to do so. They know and understand the capabilities and resourcefulness of children, and most important, they do not see this situation as unique. They believe the children made a well-considered decision not because this particular group is especially gifted in decision making, but because *all* children have the ability to listen to the perspectives of others and be careful decision makers if trusted and supported to do so.

Taking Ownership

What is your view of children? Write down ten words that describe how you see children and how they learn. You might use the sentence starter: "Children are . . ."

How do you show these ideas in your teaching? How do the children in your care know and understand that you believe these things about them? How do families know and understand your idea of the competent child? Make two columns on a piece of paper, one headed "Words" and the other headed "Actions." Write down the words and actions you use to live out your view of children as learners.

What has been revealed to you by these exercises? Are there ways you can deepen or strengthen this message?

Your View of Children with Disabilities

How does a teacher's view of children change if a child has a disability or learning difficulty? Why does the teacher's view change? If a teacher sees children as competent, then where does an image of a child having limited competencies fit? Do we see children with disabilities as also having competencies, resourcefulness, and knowledge? Do we believe they, too, have the capacity to be curious and excited about the world? Do we see how they, too, desire to be connected in relationship with others? If not, why not? Is a teacher's view of children different when a child has a disability? Should it be different?

The view many Western schooling systems hold of children with unique ways of learning (that is, "disabled") comes from a deficit model. These children are often defined and even described by what they struggle with, and not by what they are successful with. In many early learning settings, they are considered limited in their abilities and limiting to the class or school. The children are viewed as not able to learn (dis-abled), the focus is on what they cannot do or understand, and they are considered to be in *need*. Being a needy child implies they are dependent on someone else to do for them, as they cannot do for themselves. They are dependent on the teacher to teach them, and will not learn without this. This doesn't match the competent view of children at all. It is a disempowering view of children: it disempowers a child in her potential for learning, her family in believing in her child, and her teachers in creating the conditions necessary for successful learning. This can be particularly true of schools and systems focused on measuring and valuing learning through standardized and comparative testing. They see these children as a liability to their success.

Children from different cultural or social backgrounds are often similarly disadvantaged. Unconsciously, teachers view them in a similar way to children with disabilities: as less than competent. They too can be defined by their struggles or their difference rather than by what they *can* do. Worse still, this deficit view inaccurately labels children as being less than able, or even unable to learn. Expectations for them are low. For example, the native Spanish speaker learning English can be seen as less capable of learning because she does not have the English vocabulary to communicate her ideas. Often, it is accepted that a child living in a shelter will not achieve as much as others in his group purely because of the social stigma attached to his life. Sometimes, the Deaf child learning English is seen as not smart because his first language is not valued as the best way for him to communicate his thinking. In each of these examples, children are defined by their difference and not their capabilities. Many students struggling to feel successful in school learning could be better served if schools changed the view of the child from "deficient" to "holding potential," from "needy or incapable" to "resourceful and with abilities." This competent view of all children raises our expectations for them and allows us to hope and dream with them and their families, rather than setting limits on what they will achieve by not expecting very much to start with. The educators in Reggio Emilia refer to these children as having special rights, not special needs—a view that is more empowering and that conveys belief in their ability to learn and their inherent value as people (Smith 1998).

I challenge teachers to think deeply and seriously about the view they hold of children, and to ask whether their view is unconsciously different for children with disabilities. Earlier we explored how teachers' beliefs about learning directly influence the words and actions of their daily interactions with children. It is the same for a teacher's view of children with disabilities. Seeing children from a deficit or incapable view is often such a deeply hidden view that teachers are unaware of how it influences the ways they treat, respond to, and facilitate the learning of certain children. A "less than able" or "less than competent" view of a child might be unconsciously lived out when a teacher:

- assumes the child won't be able to do a particular task rather than giving her the chance to show what she can do
- focuses his planning for the child in terms of what she can't do while ignoring what she can do
- unconsciously gives the child the impression that learning is hard work and something she is not good at because most of her learning experiences are set up to focus on her "weaknesses"
- refrains from asking the child further questions that would allow him a deeper view of her thinking because he thinks she can give only a limited response
- fails to discover the child's prior knowledge and existing schema before planning, and plans an intervention program without her in mind
- sets the child up for dependency by limiting the opportunities for her to explore, discover, and learn independently, or to complete tasks independently of the teacher's involvement
- doesn't take the time to understand completely what the child is trying to communicate because he believes that her communication is limited
- only values the learning that happens while he is directing the experience, documenting and measuring the degree of support needed rather than focusing on the child's increasing independence
- only uses the child's language, literacy, and mathematical skills to determine her abilities, without exploring other ways she can show her thinking
- tells the child's family mostly about her struggles rather than her successes and competencies, so that her family begins to view the child as a deficient or incapable learner

All children benefit from learning through conversation, which is essentially learning through relationships with others, both adults and children. The conversations of all children offer teachers insight into their schema and their understandings. Certainly, the conversation of some children will challenge teachers to listen more intently and to search for other ways to understand what they are saying. But it is vital that teachers understand the importance of doing so and not assume these children have little to share or offer. Chapter 7 explores some of these ideas further through the lens of listening to the child with developing language.

Your View of Intelligence

So far, this chapter has highlighted the need to understand how you view the nature of learning. It is also important to understand how you view the nature of intelligence. Your beliefs about intelligence inform your actions and words during your conversations with children. Adults often describe a child as "smart," but what is meant by this? Being smart means different things to different people. In a broad and simple way, it can be said there are two polarized views of intelligence: fixed or malleable.

Fixed Intelligence

Do you believe intelligence is something people are born with? Do you think it remains with individuals in the same way throughout life? If you see intelligence in this way, you see it as fixed or unchangeable. In this view, a person's intelligence is not influenced by life experience; how smart a person is when he is born is how smart he remains for life. Through this view, you will see a child as either smart or not smart.

Holding a fixed view of intelligence means you define intelligence by how much knowledge a child has. You see Jules as smart because he can tell you a lot about lizards. You see Marty as not smart because he can't tell you very much about the lizards you have been learning about.

This view identifies intelligence the same way for everyone. For example, intelligence might be identified by an IQ test or a generic battery of assessment tasks. If you see intelligence in the same way for all learners, you identify it using the same means. Generic intelligence tests tend to measure intelligence through logical-mathematical or linguistic ways of thinking and expressing ideas. Being smart as defined by this fixed view means a child uses language well (and this means the primary language of the society, not necessarily the child's first language), and thinks about problems in similar ways to many other children.

Malleable Intelligence

Many educators believe intelligence is something that is used to make sense of the world, that deepens and develops during the learning process, and that comes in different forms. Ask yourself: Can a person *become* smarter? If you answer yes, then you hold a view of intelligence as malleable, or changeable and dynamic. In this view, intelligence develops through experience, interaction, and reflection.

Viewing intelligence as malleable means you are more likely to measure a child's intelligence through her ability to learn, to problem solve, and to adapt, rather than by how much she knows or how many facts she can recall. You would not favor IQ tests or packaged assessment kits to be the only or even primary means of identifying intelligence. Instead you would look at what a child can do, how she reacts to new experiences, and the connections she makes between experiences. In order to build a picture of her intelligence, you would watch how she learns and how she thinks.

Believing in the malleable nature of intelligence means you see intelligence differently in different children. Because intelligence can change over time, it also can change within an individual. Children can be intelligent in different ways. For example, Joanie shows her intelligence by being curious and asking questions about the natural world. Ali works out how to keep his block tower from collapsing. Sideik shows great empathy toward another toddler at your center who is upset or hurt, showing signs of his social and emotional intelligence. Howard Gardner's theory of multiple intelligences and Daniel Goleman's writing on social and emotional intelligence reflect this malleable nature of intelligence.

Children's Views of Intelligence

Children also possess views about intelligence, which will come as no surprise to those of us who work regularly with children. If you ask them, most children will easily name who in their learning group is "smart." A child's view of intelligence is developed through experiences and relationships and through the view of intelligence communicated through schooling experiences. This makes it essential for teachers to think carefully about the way they view intelligence and the message this view communicates to children.

Children who hold a fixed view of intelligence believe that to be smart is something you are or aren't. Because they believe they can't change whether they are smart or not, they display certain characteristic views about their learning. Their view of being smart is always focused on the end product because this represents intelligence to them. Their feelings of success are largely dependent on positive reinforcement from an adult. They don't feel good about learning unless their teacher tells them they did a good job. Such children often avoid challenges that are unfamiliar because they fear failure. Because they do not believe they can change how smart they are, they feel a sense of inadequacy and often give up when faced with a challenging situation. When involved in familiar, safe, and unchallenging tasks, their self-talk might sound something like: "I am smart enough to do this. This is easy." But when faced with a task that is unfamiliar or poses a challenge or problem, their self-talk might become: "I'm not smart enough to do this. It's too hard, and I can't do this. I'm not going to try" (Dweck 1999; Dweck and Elliott 1983).

The following conversation gives us a glimpse into how three five-year-olds see intelligence:

Lisa (adult): Can you get smarter? How?

Oscar: Yeah, you work hard and you get smart.

Tania: You do all your homework.

Jonah: You practice and practice your reading every day and you get gooder.

Oscar, Tania, and Jonah believe if they try, they can become smarter. When children view intelligence as something they can use and develop, they tend to focus not on the product but on the process of getting there. They think about the learning that happens along the way. Such children will often set goals for themselves, and show persistence in achieving these goals (Dweck 1999; Dweck and Elliott 1983). When faced with a challenging or new learning experience, their self-talk might sound like: "This is new. What can I do to work this out?" or "This is difficult, but I can work it out if I try hard."

Two-year-old Maria is another example of a child who displays many of these learning characteristics. As I watched, Maria struggled to tie her shoelaces for well over ten minutes, displaying the kind of attention span and concentration many adults do not associate with one so young. Maria set her own goal: to tie her shoelaces. In fact, she would not allow anyone to help. Maria showed great determination and persistence as she tried different strategies of looping and twisting the laces. She tested a strategy by moving her foot up and down, and when the laces parted, tried a new way. When her strategies did not produce eventual success, she did not become distraught, but simply asked me to tie them for her. Somehow she understood that she had tried everything she knew and that she needed some help for now. It is important to note that she did not feel failure. In the way that athletes set goals to improve their performance, Maria will return to her shoelaces another time. Maria's view of intelligence has been influenced by her experiences and relationships. The adults in her life have communicated their belief in her intelligence to her, and have showed her that being smart means persisting when faced with a challenge and trying different strategies to achieve a goal. Maria's intelligence is measured by her ability to learn, and in turn, she has developed dispositions to learning that will continue to deepen her intelligence over time.

Taking Ownership

How can you work out what view of intelligence you hold? Think of someone you know whom you regard as smart or intelligent. Write down the things that make you know that person is smart. What does this person do that makes you see him or her as intelligent? What do you see and hear that tells you this person is smart? Read over your list. What does this tell you about your view of intelligence?

Conclusion

The view of a competent child who constructs her own understandings from her experiences and relationships fits with a view of intelligence that is dynamic, multidimensional, and malleable. If teachers believe the most meaningful learning occurs when individuals construct their own understandings, they must challenge themselves to believe this is true for *all* human beings, no matter their age. Too often teachers pay lip service to this in their daily interactions with young learners. They say they value children's prior experience, their uniqueness, and their individual paths of learning, but then their actions betray their words by controlling children's learning choices and providing a "one size fits all" program.

However, when teachers treat each child as capable, they allow children to direct their own experiences and make some of their own decisions. In these programs, a child's voice is heard before an adult's. Teachers listen first, and are careful not to fill the day directing behavior and giving instructions to children. When children are treated as capable, they become actively engaged in learning. They ask questions, show interest, and are excited. Through their words and actions, adults teach children that they already know a lot. Children believe that their knowledge and understanding are important.

References

Dweck, C. S. 1999. *Self-Theories: Their Role in Motivation, Personality, and Development.* Philadelphia: Taylor & Francis.

Dweck, C. S., and E. Elliott. 1983. "Achievement Motivation." In *Handbook of Child Psychology,* vol.4, *Social and Personality Development,* ed. P. H. Mussen and E. M. Hetherington. New York: Wiley.

Edwards, C., L. Gandini, and G. Forman, eds. 1998. *The Hundred Languages of Children.* Greenwich, Conn.: Ablex Publishing.

Gardner, H. 1991. *The Unschooled Mind: How Children Think and How Schools Should Teach.* New York: Basic Books.

Garhart Mooney, C. 2000. *Theories of Childhood: An Introduction to Dewy, Montessori, Erikson, Piaget, and Vygotsky.* St. Paul: Redleaf Press.

Goleman, D. 1995. *Emotional Intelligence: Why It Can Matter More Than I.Q.* New York: Bantam Books.

Jensen, E. 2005. *Teaching with the Brain in Mind.* Alexandria, Va.: ASCD.

Owocki, G. 1999. *Literacy through Play.* Portsmouth, N.H.: Heinemann.

Ritchhart, R. 2002. *Intellectual Character: What It Is, Why It Matters, and How to Get It.* San Francisco: Jossey-Bass.

Sacks, O. 1990. *Seeing Voices.* New York: Vintage Books.

Smith, C. 1998. "Children with 'Special Rights' in the Preprimary Schools and Infant-Toddler Centers of Reggio Emilia." In *The Hundred Languages of Children*, ed. C. Edwards, L. Gandini, and G. Forman. Westport, Conn.: Ablex Publishing.

Vygotsky, L. S. 1978. *Mind in Society: The Development of Higher Psychological Processes.* Cambridge, Mass.: Harvard University Press.

CHAPTER TWO

Conversations in the Educational Setting

Now that you have spent time refining your view of children and articulating your personal theories of learning, it is time to consider the types of conversations you want to nurture in order to live out this vision for learning. In this chapter we'll look both at the characteristics of conversations that help children learn, and the types of conversational moments that take place in educational settings. This will help you to imagine the conversations that will take place in your setting, and to begin making plans for them.

It is important to be clear about the characteristics of conversations that most effectively engage young learners. Not all kinds of talk will suffice: giving directions may teach children how to follow instructions but will not engage them in thinking about their ideas. If you only ask questions that seek one right answer, children will not be engaged in interactions that stretch their schema about the world. Conversations engage the thinking of young learners when they have these characteristics:

- Learners' voices are heard the most.
- Teacher talk seeks to discover children's ideas.
- Children talk with each other.
- Children have time to think.
- Topics connect to children's interests, explorations, and questions.
- Conversations are documented and interpreted to reveal thinking.
- Conversations are used to stretch children's thinking.

Learners' Voices Are Heard the Most

Courtney B. Cazden's research (1988) found that many American classrooms are dominated by teacher talk, where teacher-student interaction is characterized by this process:

1. Teacher initiates by calling on specific student.
2. Child provides a response.
3. Teacher comments on the response.

The study found this was the most dominant form of conversation in all grades. Not only was the teacher doing the majority of the talking, but the teacher also controlled who spoke and when. In addition, little interaction between students was noted. While this study was conducted back in 1988, my recent experience in schools has provided evidence that not very much has changed.

Teachers don't always want it to be this way. There is a current swing back to teacher-dominated talk in many learning environments because of the pressure on teachers to "cover the curriculum" and "make sure the children know this stuff to pass the test." Sadly, with each year this push seems to be moving more and more into the learning environments of young children, and child care teachers and home-based caregivers are feeling the pressure to "teach," and, subsequently, to dominate conversations in ways more usually seen in elementary settings.

Teacher Talk Seeks to Discover Children's Ideas

Teacher talk within a culture of conversation is intended to foster growth, independence, and learning. In these settings, teachers talk in order to stretch young learners' thinking and understanding about themselves and about the world, and not in order to test children's knowledge or control their thinking and actions. It is the difference between a monologue delivered *at* children, and a dialogue *with* them.

Teacher talk that only seeks one right answer is called *closed*. It will not reveal a child's rich schema about a topic. For example, while a child is playing with toy animals, closed teacher talk might sound something like this:

Teacher:	What animal is this?
Ruth:	Horse.
Teacher:	Right! What color is it?
Ruth:	Black.
Teacher:	Yes, but can you see another color too?
Ruth:	White too.

Teacher talk that instead seeks to gain an insight into a child's prior knowledge and experience would use *open-ended* questions and comments to bring out more information. An open-ended conversation in the same situation might sound something like this:

Teacher: What's happening here?

Billy: Horse is running . . .

Teacher: Oh, what else?

Billy: The boy wants to go on the horse but the horse run away.

Teacher: What will happen?

Billy: He waits and his daddy will get the horse. See? [shows the teacher a toy man representing the daddy]

Teacher: How will the daddy get the horse? It's running so fast.

Billy: The rope on the horse and the horse is tired and the daddy . . . he puts the rope on and the boy he gets on the horse.

In the first conversation, the teacher's questioning gave very little information about Ruth's thinking or knowledge about horses. The questions were closed and looked for very specific answers from Ruth. Her answers were either right or wrong. Ruth's teacher learned that Ruth can recognize a horse and knows some colors.

However, the second conversation reveals much more about Billy's schema. His teacher's open-ended questions were aimed at finding out as much as possible about Billy's knowledge of the animals he was playing with. The teacher learned that Billy has such understandings as: horses run fast, people ride horses, daddies help fix problems that are too big for children, and a rope can be used to get a horse. The conversation also sparked the teacher's curiosity. He had questions about Billy's schema to explore further: Is Billy's rope a lasso or a rein? Has Billy been horseback riding himself? Does Billy see his dad as someone who can fix lots of problems? What else does Billy know about riding horses? The open-ended questions such as "How will the daddy get the horse?" provoked Billy to stretch his thinking. This conversation is far more effective at gaining insight into Billy's prior knowledge. It shows interest in his ideas and it fosters learning. It also allows Billy his independent thought: the answers were Billy's, not those already in his teacher's mind, and gave Billy's teacher much more information about Billy's unique understanding of the world. He had more information about Billy to plan a curriculum with Billy in mind.

By asking closed questions, Ruth's teacher found out that Ruth can name some colors. This might be new information for the teacher and adds to what she knows about Ruth. However, it is a very limiting understanding of Ruth as a learner. It defines Ruth's ability as a learner by what she knows and can say back to the teacher. This is an example of seeing learning as the ability to copy what the teacher does, as discussed in chapter 1. On the other hand, the conversation between Billy and his teacher built a wider understanding of Billy as a learner. The open-ended questions reveal Billy's ability to imagine, to problem solve, and to use his prior knowledge in his play, and therefore his ability to learn.

Children Talk with Each Other

In order to engage learners, conversation needs to include opportunities for children to talk with each other while they are learning, as well as opportunities to talk with adults. As Cazden's research showed, in many classrooms the emphasis is on teacher-learner-teacher conversations. These interactions do not provide opportunities for social learning, in which children hear the different ideas and perspectives of their friends and are able to connect them with their own understanding.

The following transcript from a conversation between four-year-olds shows the rich social learning that happens when children have the opportunity to talk with each other and not just with the teacher. The teacher gave the children time to talk among themselves without interrupting them with teacher talk that may have brought the children's talk to a halt. The children had just found a bug in their room and ran to their teacher with the news.

Teacher:	What shall we do about the bug?
Jimmy:	I have a bug vacuum. I caught two beetles but we let them go.
Hannah:	How did you get them inside?
Jimmy:	The vacuum has a kind of a gun.
Hannah:	Maybe it got under the crack?
Jimmy:	The best thing about the bug vacuum is that my brother got it for his birthday and it's very, very cool.
Melina:	Ladybugs can fly. When I was in Sonya's car, a ladybug sat on my car.
Hannah:	Is a butterfly a bug?
Lauren:	Yes! It is! We saw ants outside.
Jimmy:	We're going to be ant explorers.

The children's ideas in this conversation bounce off each other. They don't need the teacher to probe or prod to bring their ideas out because they can do this for themselves. Jimmy connects the bug in the classroom with his home experience and this sparks Hannah's curiosity. Because her teacher does not interrupt, Hannah is able to ask her questions freely and follow them up until she is satisfied with her understanding. Melina isn't so interested in Jimmy's bug vacuum, but connects to her own experience and knowledge of bugs. Again, her teacher gives her the opportunity to do so by staying out of it. She doesn't interrupt or direct the conversation back to Jimmy's bug vacuum, or back to the original question. Because she does this, Hannah has a new question to ask, and Lauren engages in the conversation because she knows with authority that butterflies are bugs. It doesn't matter that the children are yet to come up with an answer to the initial question from the teacher, "What shall we do about the bug?" because the children are engaged in working it out by connecting to their prior knowledge. By not interrupting or taking over the conversation, this teacher gives the young learners the time and the freedom to connect with things that are important to them. They are engaged in learning together, engaged in rich social learning.

When children are encouraged and supported to talk with each other, not just back and forth with the teacher, they see their ideas are important. They are more willing to share their thinking in future conversations because they know they are listened to and their ideas are important to their friends. The more young learners that participate in conversation, the more opportunities they have to use language for authentic purposes. The more they use language, the more they practice using new words and skills for learning, and the more these skills will develop. This is not a cycle of failure or disengagement but a cycle of engagement and, therefore, a cycle of successful learning.

Children Have Time to Think

Mary Budd Rowe first introduced the idea of a wait time in the 1970s (1987). Rowe's research clearly showed the benefits of allowing silence in terms of the quality and quantity of learner responses. With thinking time, learners gave longer and more "correct" responses, they decreased the amount of "I don't know" replies, and more students participated in discussion. I prefer, like Robert Stahl, to call this wait time, "thinking time." It more accurately describes what is happening and conveys an important message as to the purpose of the silence. That is, to think about the topic, not to just sit. By allowing for this thinking time, you communicate that thinking is important—important enough to be given time. It also allows young learners the time needed to take in information from others, whether it is information from the teacher or an idea from another child. We all benefit from time to process information, reflect on it, and make connections to our own thinking.

Conversation needs to have a relaxed pace in which young learners have the time to think, reflect, and share their ideas with one another.

Taking Ownership

Be more conscious of the silence in conversations. Are you allowing children time to think before they are expected to respond? Set a goal for yourself to silently count to three before asking the next question or making the next comment. How does this feel? Do you see any changes in the children's behavior or contributions as a result of this thinking time?

Topics Connect to Children's Interests, Explorations, and Questions

What do you like to talk about? My guess would be that you enjoy and feel most confident talking about topics that are important to you and that you feel you know something about. Imagine how you would feel if someone asked you to join a conversation about the current political state of Laos. If you know something about this topic, or perhaps have been to Laos and have an interest in learning more about what is happening there, you would likely feel comfortable and engage in a rich discussion. On the other hand, if you are not familiar with the country or its political realities, you would be less likely to engage. You might be bored, irritated, or confused; the conversation might fall flat or simply proceed without you.

Young learners act the same way. They feel more comfortable and confident when participating in conversations about topics that are important to them: their interests, their lives, and their daily experiences. These are topics that they know something about so they will have ideas and experiences to bring to the conversation. Simply put, they will have something to say.

Remember Anthony? He is continually asking questions in a search for information about the way the world works. These are the questions that are important to him. When his schooling did not give him the opportunity to explore his questions, he shut down and became disinterested. He was interested in understanding how sight works, but his school experience did not tap into his questions or interests. There were other questions presented to Anthony, but these were set by his teacher and not by him. "How do caterpillars change?" his teacher asked after a series of lessons about the life cycle of butterflies. Anthony already knew about caterpillars becoming butterflies long before he began kindergarten, so he was not invested in answering his teacher's question. He didn't care and he disengaged. Anthony was, in fact, curious about the life cycle of butterflies, and had his own questions. He was interested in finding answers to *those questions.* He really wanted to know "What is the cocoon made out of?" "Does it hurt when the butterfly breaks out of the cocoon?" and "What do they eat inside the cocoon?" Unfortunately, Anthony was never given the opportunity to explore these personally important questions. If he had been supported to actively explore his own questions and tap into his natural curiosity, he would have been far more engaged and invested in his learning.

Conversations Are Documented and Interpreted to Reveal Thinking

Documenting conversations means capturing and collecting them in a permanent way. Recording conversations, videotaping them, or writing them down are ways to document conversations. When conversations are documented they become more tangible. Scribing children's words, for example, makes their thinking more visible for teachers and for their families. Children see that their words have importance because their teacher takes the time to write them down. Families see that their children's ideas are important because the teacher records them and displays them carefully in the learning environment.

When children's words are written down they are no longer temporary, but become words that can be returned to again and again. This strengthens the visibility of the children's learning because with each rereading or reviewing of a conversation, more insights can be made. It may not be until you have read a transcript three times that you see a connection a child is making. During the actual conversation, you may be so focused on managing the group that you miss what a child says. Returning to the documentation allows you another opportunity to listen intently. It is a gift of another chance to think carefully about what a child is saying and thinking. The most powerful way to interpret the meaning behind a child's words is to be with colleagues or the child's family. The documented conversation, therefore, allows those who may not have been present at the initial conversation to participate in the interpretation and meaning-making process.

Conversations Are Used to Stretch Children's Thinking

Conversations are opportunities to engage children in constructing their understandings. They provide the time and place for intellectual conflict, from other children's ideas or from questions asked by the teacher. The interpretation that happens away from the conversation is another place you can plan for learning experiences that will stretch children's thinking. The great value in documenting and interpreting conversations is that this collaborative process leads teachers to decisions about further learning experiences. This is an example of planning curriculum with the child in mind. The documentation reveals some of the children's prior knowledge and understanding to you, and you ask, "What learning experiences could I provide to stretch this understanding?" Conversations can lead to further conversations to delve deeper into children's emerging theories. These new conversations give you a better understanding about what they think. Or they can lead to other experiences, such as a field trip, working with new materials, or reading a book about the topic. These new experiences provide children with a new context for their social learning. Their thinking is stretched by new experiences and different conversations within these new contexts. The cycle of engaged learning spirals and evolves, all within a curriculum planned with unique learners in mind.

Creating Conversational Moments

Teachers who develop a culture of conversation in their learning environments do so purposefully because they know and understand the importance of talking and of listening to the learning process. They understand that children need environments, time, and opportunities to talk with each other and with adults. They know to truly honor the prior learning and developing schema of young learners they need to plan purposefully to listen intently to the children. (Environmental considerations, including scheduling issues, will be explored more fully in chapter 3.) Conversations in an educational setting fall into two main categories: spontaneous and facilitated. In order to create a culture of conversation and engage children in this spiraling process of learning, you will need to plan for them to be involved in both kinds of talking and listening.

Spontaneous Conversations

Spontaneous conversations are those that happen naturally during the course of the day while children are engaged in various experiences. When thinking about children's language, we often focus on planned experiences, missing the richness of the unplanned conversations that occur throughout the day. Spontaneous conversations do require planning and forethought. They require planning for materials, space, time, and experiences in which children will work together rather than alone and will engage in conversation while immersed in the social context of learning.

Becoming aware of the richness of conversation during block play (where, for example, three kindergarten children are creating a castle) or at the painting easels (where two children are showing each other how to mix colors to create just the right shade of blue) opens up new opportunities for listening intently to children. Mealtimes, snacktimes, and the precious time as children enter the room in the morning also offer time for spontaneous conversation. Mealtimes are a delightful time to informally chat with children or to listen as they talk with each other. The topics of conversation are often very interesting and illuminating.

In spontaneous conversation, the topic is always decided by the children, and the script is created and directed by them as well. The teacher will often (but not always) sit outside these conversations, participating only when and if she is invited.

Creating opportunities for children to work in pairs or small groups provides great opportunity for spontaneous talk and social learning. Children are more likely to be relaxed and open when talking spontaneously with their friends and, in particular, while they are engaged in active learning. For example, some children do not have the confidence to contribute to a whole-class conversation or when questioned by the teacher about something in particular. During conversations that are more spontaneous and connected to their social learning experiences, however, they often feel more confident and open to talk.

One of my greatest joys when visiting early learning environments is eavesdropping on two reading buddies who are discussing the book they are reading. By structuring the day to include both reading and talking time, you can gain insight into the thinking of two young readers that may not be visible through a written response or when they are talking to an adult. For example, let's eavesdrop on Minh and Kiah.

Minh:	The book is about . . .
Kiah:	A girl writing a picture about everything she sees . . . she's imagining the pictures.
Minh:	Maybe she wants to be an artist?
Kiah:	I remember when I was a little baby, I was a girl like this and I was bothering my Mom for crayons . . .
Minh:	I wanted to be a drawer and this book has the same feeling. Drawing—drawing. Art—art. [points from the book to herself]
Kiah:	Me too. I want to be an artist when I grow up too.
Minh:	You want to be an artist too?

This delightful conversation shows the value of providing opportunity for spontaneous conversation. Minh and Kiah's conversation allowed them to connect with their reading in new ways because their individual experience and ideas interacted with each other. Reading the book alone might have led to some of these connections, but it was the conversation that brought out these ideas. Talking with each other enabled the girls' ideas to more fully form because they were spoken aloud. They used their language to organize their thinking. When Kiah shares the connection she makes between the book and her life, it sparks the same connection-making in Minh.

Spontaneous conversation made these connections possible. The girls were not directed to talk about a specific topic or idea. The teacher gave them the time in a relaxed schedule with plenty of space for spontaneous conversation; the specific topic was their decision. Allowing children to talk about things that are important to them engages them in learning because they are interested and invested in the conversation. When children are able to talk about what they are doing *while* they are doing it, they find authentic purpose to participate in conversation and in learning. Young children have a real reason to be in conversation with each other, and therefore will be more fully engaged in their learning. Making time and space for spontaneous conversation will provide this for them.

Facilitated Conversations

Facilitated conversations offer different benefits for children's learning than do spontaneous ones. The purpose of this time is to talk and listen to ideas around a particular topic of interest to the group. This differs from spontaneous talk, where the purpose for talking is more closely linked to the experience (such as to paint, to build, or to bid farewell to friends in the afternoon) and the topic is decided by the children involved. In facilitated conversation, the teacher takes a more active role and enters the conversation with a specific purpose in mind. Rather than sitting outside the conversation, eavesdropping on the spontaneous talk of the learners, the teacher becomes one of the participants, guiding the conversation. She may have planned to talk about a particular topic and prepared questions to help guide the conversation. She may have brought an object of interest for the group to talk about. She may pick up on a topic the children are spontaneously talking about and choose to become involved in the conversation.

Facilitated conversations are important times for you to listen to children and discover their prior knowledge, ideas, or confusions about a topic. You will get some of this insight from spontaneous conversation also, but in a facilitated conversation you will be able to purposefully search deeper into children's ideas. Facilitated conversations provide the opportunity to explore an idea more deeply, and to connect thinking from previous days. You can help children make connections between experiences and ideas that occur over time because you take a more active role in facilitated conversations.

These conversations also allow for the creation of intellectual conflict, and therefore they can shift the children's thinking or challenge their existing schema. There will be moments of intellectual conflict during spontaneous conversations, but facilitated ones give you more power to bring out children's different opinions and ideas.

Here is a typical early childhood story to illustrate this. After listening to spontaneous conversations in the block area while children worked to create a city, the teacher gained some insight into their prior knowledge about building. She decides to have a facilitated conversation with the small group of children, and introduce some intellectual conflict to their ideas. She gathers the builders together and helps them remember the city they built with apartment buildings, a hospital, and a grocery store. "I was wondering about a couple of things about your city," she begins. "How do the people get from the grocery store to their apartment building? Where do the children play in your city?" The facilitated conversation allows the teacher to ask questions that will create intellectual conflict and challenge the children's thinking. Her questions, which are appropriate and purposeful in a facilitated conversation, also act as a catalyst for further social learning by the city builders. Because of this conversation, the children continue their construction, creating roads complete with traffic lights and cars. One child creates a park with paper and crayons.

Three kinds of facilitated conversations are critical in early childhood environments:

- whole-group conversations
- small-group conversations
- one-to-one conversations

WHOLE-GROUP CONVERSATIONS

It is important to plan for whole-group conversations during your day. Gathering your whole group of young learners together creates a sense of community. Building in time for predictable whole-group conversation times gives young learners a feeling of security. If each and every day they are invited to talk about their ideas and experiences and to listen to those of their classmates, they will learn that conversation is a natural and important part of learning. The benefits of whole-class conversations include:

- Children's schemas are stretched by listening to the experiences and ideas of others.
- Children are drawn into conversation by listening to others' ideas and experiences.
- Children use their talk to organize their learning and take roles of responsibility for setting up their learning environment.
- Teachers discover possibilities for future learning experiences from listening to children's ideas.
- Teachers have a predictable and familiar environment for facilitating conversations about a particular topic of interest.
- Children and teachers have a regular and planned structure for conversation through which to connect learning experiences that may otherwise remain isolated events.

One of the most common whole-group meetings is commonly known as the morning meeting. Many early learning settings implement morning meetings as a way to begin the day, to settle the children as a group, and to prepare for the day ahead. This time offers wonderful opportunities for facilitated conversations. Teachers can listen carefully for possibilities for further learning that are sparked by news shared by children during the morning meeting. Responding immediately to those things that are important to the children engages them in meaningful learning. Morning meetings offer the perfect time for this because the teacher has the rest of the day to respond to or have further conversations with children to explore their ideas.

Morning meetings also provide a time and place for teachers to activate children's prior knowledge about a topic the group will explore. Because learning begins with prior knowledge, creating time for children to open up their prior knowledge through conversation gives the experience greater meaning for the learner. This in turn creates greater engagement on the part of the children. For example, the teacher might plan for small groups of children to bake cookies during the day. During morning meeting, the teacher can facilitate a conversation to activate children's prior knowledge about cookie baking. Talking with each other about cookie baking will make the small-group experience much more meaningful. It also allows the teacher to gain greater insight into the children's prior knowledge and vocabulary associated with cookie baking. The teacher will learn which words the children know and are using, which allows her to better choose which words she will embed in her conversation to stretch their vocabularies.

Morning meetings also allow young learners to take on roles of responsibility for establishing the learning environment. Conversations during the morning meeting can help children make choices about what they want to explore, what materials they will need, and who they will work with. A facilitated conversation for this purpose supports children in making decisions for themselves about their learning. This makes the learning more meaningful and relevant to them. At the same time, children are using language to organize their thinking and organize their learning.

It is also helpful to create time for an afternoon meeting, which I sometimes call a reflection meeting. The afternoon meeting may not need to be as long as the morning meeting. Five or ten minutes may suffice. By gathering as a learning group and sharing experiences and learning from the day, children learn skills and strategies for remembering, reflecting, and planning (essential tools for lifelong learning). Learning to reflect, evaluate, and plan for learning is often associated with older students, but young learners are far more capable of this than they are given credit for, when they are given frequent opportunities to remember and reflect on real and meaningful experiences.

During the reflection meeting, children once more have the opportunity to use their language to organize their thinking. In addition to talking about their prior knowledge and experience or their ideas about a topic, they can also talk about their learning. During a reflection meeting, teachers can ask questions such as: How did the day go? What problems did you solve? What did you learn about or think about today? What are you interested in exploring tomorrow? The reflection meeting allows children to learn from the experiences of others, to have their thinking stretched by listening to different ideas, and to begin planning for future experiences. Teachers gain insight into children's experiences and interests and receive valuable information for planning future learning experiences or topics of conversation. Like morning meetings, reflection meetings create cohesiveness as the learning group begins and ends each day together.

Teachers Dawn and Vanessa use these meeting ideas to strengthen their kindergartners' learning during investigation time (also called choice time or work time). After several weeks at school, Dawn and Vanessa observed that the children continued to "float" among the learning centers, or would follow each other from area to area without a clear purpose. They wanted the children's play to deepen in complexity and last longer, and their use of language to become more complex.

Dawn, Vanessa, and I discussed ways to ensure that the materials in the centers were connected to the children's interests and prior experiences, both in school and at home. We also decided to implement brief before and after investigation-time meetings.

The purpose of the before meeting was to connect children with their experiences from the previous day, or with ideas they had been discussing with teachers at the morning meeting. They made plans for what they would work on during investigation time, decided on the materials they would need, and helped the teachers prepare materials and spaces.

The purpose of the after meeting was to share what had happened during investigation time, and for the teachers to help the children connect it to the plans they made earlier. The teachers did not insist that children follow their plans completely, but felt that it was important to help the children see the connection between planning, action, and reflection. Children shared what they had been making, exploring, and playing, and their ideas about their play. If a longer-term project was underway, the children and teachers would discuss its progress, whether it would continue, and what materials or support was needed next.

At both meetings, children often showed their work, stretching the ideas of other children by their model and explanation of their painting, collage, block construction, or puzzle. Rather than create a set agenda or routine for these meetings, Dawn and Vanessa facilitated the conversations based on the ideas presented by the children either during the meeting or while they were working during investigation time.

Within only two weeks of implementing these before and after meetings, Dawn and Vanessa observed five significant changes to their kindergartners' play.

1. Children demonstrated greater respect for one another's work.

   The children's block constructions were always kept up rather than packed away each day, but the teachers were frustrated that the children would frequently knock them down as they moved about the room. After implementing the meetings, the children seemed to have more respect for the block constructions made by others and rarely were the structures knocked down, even accidentally. The teachers theorized that because the children heard the story of the constructions during the meetings, the children understood them in new ways, understood the work involved in creating them, and felt more connected to the work of others. They now had an investment in the constructions and so shared the responsibility of caring for them.

2. Children were more deeply engaged and spent longer time in specific play areas.

   Children now stayed in one area far longer and did not flit from one center to another as they had done previously. Teachers also noticed that the children got into their play and learning much faster than before. They believed it was a result of talking, planning, and rehearsing their play in their minds during the before meeting. Children went to the areas with greater purpose and an established idea of what their play was to be about.

3. Children interacted more with one another, and cooperative play increased.

   Children in the block area and imaginative play area showed a dramatic increase in cooperative play, whereas previously much of their play had been parallel (side-by-side playing and not explicitly connected in ideas or interactions). Dramatic play became an area for birthday parties and for acting out familiar storybooks. The players had more defined roles and a more cohesive theme to their play. In the block area, children moved from building different individual structures to creating one large structure with a cohesive theme. Again, Dawn and Vanessa believed this was the result of the planning and sharing during the before meeting.

4. Groups of children began to build on the play of others.

   In the block area, new groups of children would choose to keep the existing structures and build onto them, rather than starting from scratch with a new construction. In the dramatic play area, new groups of players chose to continue playing with similar themes and narratives to those they heard about from the previous day's players. Because they shared their learning and their ideas in the after meeting, the class as a whole was more connected and invested in each other's play and learning. In future weeks, the block area became a combined class construction of Spider-Man, and the dramatic play area hosted many variations of *Bunny Cakes* by Rosemary Wells, one of the class's favorite storybooks.

5. Children began to seek help from one another rather than only from the teachers.

Observational drawing of different flower varieties was a regular learning experience for these kindergartners, and when Leo, a student, wanted to create just the right shade of pink for the rose he was drawing, he experimented with color mixing with watercolors. This was shared and celebrated at the after meeting, with Leo demonstrating how he achieved the color. The next day, two children asked Leo to help them mix colors so they could create their desired shades also. From that day on, Leo became the class expert in color mixing.

These five points are powerful indicators of engaged learning. Can you visualize the children at work in this class? They are active learners who use materials, talk with each other, and ask the teachers questions. Some children are laughing. Some are seriously intent on their task. The decision to facilitate conversations before and after investigation time led to engaged and meaningful learning for these kindergartners. Because people tend to talk about things that are important to them, the children's conversations gave greater importance and value to all the other learning experiences that were happening in Dawn and Vanessa's class. The conversations became the thread that connected the children's learning and that connected them with each other.

Taking Ownership

When do you gather your whole-group of young learners together? Do they come together for a circle time of games and songs? Do you bring them together as a group each day for story time? Do the children share their news during a news time or morning talk?

- *How much of this whole-group time is teacher talk? How much is child talk?*
- *What do you talk about during these times?*
- *What do children talk about during these times?*
- *What is the purpose of the talk you are engaged in? Are the children organizing their learning or thinking? Are you organizing the day? Are you giving instructions? Are children sharing their experiences with others? Are you giving information?*

Becoming aware of what you are doing and the purpose for the talk you are already engaged in with young learners is the first step in developing a deeper understanding of the role of conversation in learning.

SMALL-GROUP CONVERSATIONS

Not all facilitated conversations should involve the whole class. Many of the benefits of small-group conversations are the same as those of whole-group conversations, but it is often more efficient, effective, and beneficial to structure and plan for small-group conversations. The benefits of facilitating conversations in small groups include:

- allow for greater participation by more children
- easier to facilitate
- easier to delve deeper into children's ideas
- provide closer links for children between conversation and experiences that explore an idea further
- create a safe environment for children unsure of large-group conversations

Small-group conversations allow for greater participation by more children. Children in a small group have more airtime, and in this setting, the teacher is better able to dig into the children's ideas and follow their thinking more closely.

In addition, it is often easier for a teacher to facilitate a small-group conversation than a whole-class conversation, so it may be a more successful way for you to start developing skills in facilitating and questioning. It is easier to keep track of the ideas of four or five children than a group of twenty. It is also easier to provide four children with enough time to talk than it is with a larger group. Many teachers feel more confident that they can listen to all the children's ideas in a small group.

Small-group conversations allow you to pick up on the interests of particular learners more effectively because you have more time with a smaller number of children. For example, from your morning meetings you may have noticed the same three or four children have been talking for the past few days about jumping in puddles while wearing their new boots. Rather than continue exploring these ideas with the whole class when you suspect the rest of the children are not as invested in the topic, you could structure a time and place to meet with this small group and continue exploring their ideas.

At the same time, before assuming some children are not interested in a particular topic that has been introduced to your whole group, it is helpful to facilitate some small-group conversations, particularly for children who rarely express their ideas in a whole-class meeting. Even when teachers go to great lengths to create a culture of conversation and a climate of security, there are learners who do not participate fully in whole-class meetings. What looks like disinterest may actually be lack of confidence to share ideas in a large group. Smaller groups, even in pairs or individually with teachers, make it easier for these children to share their ideas more confidently.

Often this small-group setting is a more effective way of linking the conversation to other learning areas, such as suggesting children could draw or construct their ideas. It is often a tighter fit for young learners to go from a small-group conversation to a connected experience such as drawing. Their ideas often get lost in between a whole-class conversation and an invitation to participate in a specific experience. For example, after talking with a small group about the new shoes they are wearing, listening to their stories of their feet being measured, and trying on different types of shoes, you can invite them to draw what it was like in the shoe store or what it looked like when their foot was being measured. You can also suggest they convert the dramatic play area into a shoe store, and help them plan what they will need in the store and the kinds of materials they could use to make these items.

ONE-TO-ONE CONVERSATIONS

It is also important to plan time to talk one-to-one with individual children. Again, many of the opportunities for learning in conversation found in whole-group and small-group conversations will be present. But like small-group meetings, one-to-one conversations give you the chance to explore more deeply and more intimately with one child. You may choose to facilitate a one-to-one conversation because:

- You want to develop a closer relationship with a child new to your program, or with a child you have not connected with yet.
- You are curious to discover more about an experience or idea the child shared at a whole-group or small-group conversation.
- The child's family has shared a concern, a fear, or other news with you, and you want to explore this with the child. It is particularly important to be aware of the need for privacy if the topic is of a sensitive nature—this situation requires a one-to-one conversation.

- You want to support a child who is experiencing a difficult time. Spending extra quality time with him tells him how important he is.
- You are interested in learning more about a child's process of learning or thinking, and so need to talk with her while she is engaged in the learning experience, such as while she is painting or while she is at the water table.
- A child is being ostracized by other children and you want to show him he is important to you and to the group. One-to-one time also allows you to model positive attitudes and interactions with the child for any "eavesdropping" children.

This being said, it is also important to respect those times when children do not wish to speak to you. For example, the creative process of drawing a newly constructed palace of blocks may be too absorbing to be broken by talk.

A word about reading, writing, and math conferences in elementary schools. These one-to-one conversations are often planned by teachers to talk specifically with a child about his literacy or mathematical thinking. Through each conversation, teachers learn information about the child that they may not get from a larger group conversation. Again, you can use this time to delve more deeply into a child's thinking, and you can also relate the conversation directly to a book he is reading, a story he is writing, or a puzzle he is solving. Conferences are also opportunities for teaching, and as such can become quite teacher-directed and teacher-led. This usually means more teacher talk and less learner talk. It is important to also hold conferences where the learner does most of the talking.

When I hold a conference, I always begin by listening to the learner and asking about his current work, such as the book he is writing or the symmetrical design he is creating. Only by first listening to the learner can I determine what I might teach him during this time. Or I may get information that leads me to the decision to teach something at another time, rather than take the airtime away from the child at that moment. You will learn so much about children by observing them in the active process of learning: watching them paint, listening to them read, or observing their problem solving when making a repetitive color-block pattern. But how do you get inside their heads and discover what they are thinking about as they read, write, or problem solve? What thinking strategies are they using to help them in the learning task? Do they have a particular plan? By engaging in conversation, asking questions, and then listening closely to what the learner says, you can gain insight into his inner world.

Taking Ownership

Choose a week to put the spotlight on conversations the children are already engaged in. Give yourself some time to discover what the children already know and already do in conversations with each other and with you. This will build a picture of your current experience and help you determine a starting place for extending or deepening conversations in your program. It might be helpful to choose a different lens for the spotlight each day, looking and listening to one of the following for a day at a time:

- *conversations the children have with each other while they are playing, building, and creating*
- *conversations the children have with adults while playing, building, or creating, or during group times*
- *conversations during which children plan and organize their work*
- *conversations during which children share their experiences*
- *conversations during which children share their ideas about the world*

Keep a notebook and pencil handy to jot down what you see and hear. Where are the conversations happening? What time of the day? Who is involved? What, generally, are they talking about?

At the end of the day, take ten minutes to read through your notes and think about the conversations as a whole, rather than as a series of isolated experiences. What is happening? How are children using conversation? What patterns do you notice? Write a couple of sentences to journal your overall feeling about how the children are using different types of conversation for learning.

At the end of the week, you will have built a picture of conversations in your early learning environment. Read through your notes and documentation and reflect on the week as a whole:

- *Are there patterns of conversations emerging?*
- *What do you notice about the kinds of conversations the children are having?*
- *What do you notice about how the children are using their talk to help them learn?*
- *Has anything surprised you about this picture of your week?*

The First Step

Creating a culture of conversation in your setting requires commitment and action. Often taking the action (and keeping it consistent) proves most challenging. When making changes, start small so you will feel a sense of control and a feeling of success. Trying to do it all at once is likely to leave you feeling overwhelmed, and perhaps even discourage you from implementing some changes. Teachers embracing a pedagogical change sometimes say "I tried that but it didn't work" or "That won't work with my kids." Often the reality is that it *will* work, but either the new structure, routine, or behavior has not been given enough time to become a habit and therefore hasn't integrated with the culture of the setting, or a teacher has tried to do too much too quickly and has been overwhelmed by the changes. Culture takes time and consistent practice to build, but if you are confident and clear about the pedagogical beliefs driving your practice, you will choose to continue the path begun and not change course.

Meet with your colleagues and talk about what you believe about children's learning. Together, make a list of your beliefs about how conversation supports learning and how you can plan for this with the children. Display this for families so your beliefs and values are made visible and shared. Think about your day and be more conscious of how you create conversational moments that can be both spontaneous and facilitated, and work on making these a regular daily part of the learning life of your group. Think about the children's prior knowledge and experience, and plan ways to learn more about this. These strategies will set you well on the road to creating a strong culture of conversation and engaging the children in their learning.

References

Cazden, C. B. 1988. *Classroom Discourse: The Language of Teaching and Learning.* Portsmouth, N.H.: Heinemann.

Rowe, Mary Budd. 1987. "Wait Time: Slowing Down May Be a Way of Speeding Up." *American Educator* 11 (spring).

Stahl, R. J. 1994. *Using "Think-Time" and "Wait-Time" Skillfully in the Classroom.* Indiana: ERIC Clearinghouse for Social Studies/Social Science Education.

CHAPTER THREE

Creating the Right Environments for Conversations

Conversations are best nurtured and developed within environments that encourage open sharing and active listening. The wise teacher understands how the physical space, the schedule, and the climate interact to give children the opportunity to talk and listen to each other, and also to feel safe and comfortable to share their ideas. This chapter will explore the role played by the physical space of your learning environment, and then discuss how to structure conversations throughout your day. Finally, we will explore ways to establish a climate that nurtures and supports conversations for learning.

Physical Environment

Have you ever felt overwhelmed when entering a large department store or one of those huge discount stores? Can you recall how it looked and how you felt entering one of these stores?

Picture yourself surrounded by rack after rack of clothes squashed together and shelves of shoes, bags, and all sorts of must-haves piled on top of each other. When you left home, you probably had a particular purpose for your shopping trip—perhaps a list of items that you needed to purchase. But when you find this jumble of items, you feel confused and anxious, and forget for a moment what you're there for. You don't know where to go or what to do first. There are people everywhere, pushing and shoving past each other to get to that prized item they had their eye on. Loud music fights to be heard over the even louder din of hundreds of shoppers.

What a nightmare! You try to find that item on your list amongst a pile of things on a table, but it is so jumbled that you need to spend an hour sorting through the pile to have any chance of success. All you feel is anxiety, stress, and annoyance at not being able to find what you need. The crowd is irritating, and people's behavior is, quite frankly, rude. You start to ask yourself why you came to this store in the first place, and just want to leave. The purpose of your shopping trip takes second place to restoring some sense of peace and order to your day.

So what relationship does a cluttered store have to creating an environment for conversation? Each environment conveys powerful messages to those who enter it. Imagine for a moment that you enter a kindergarten classroom. The first thing you see is a teacher's desk in the front corner of the room. Behind the desk is a blackboard, and it faces individual desks and chairs arranged in rows. Without looking any further, this environment has already communicated a message. What kinds of interactions do you imagine in this environment? Who controls the talking in this classroom? Do children have opportunities to learn with and from each other?

The clutter in the store gives the message that the items for sale are not important or valuable because no care is taken to how they are stored and organized. The disarray conveys that the shoppers are not important or valued because no consideration is given to making their shopping experience easy and enjoyable. In the same way, the choices you make in preparing your learning environment give children and families powerful messages about what is important to you. A designated space for your whole group to meet will show everyone you value opportunities to be together and that it is important for young children to meet as a whole group. The spaces you create for block play or painting, for example, and how you arrange the materials within these spaces, will convey how important these types of learning are in your program.

Think about the feelings experienced by the shoppers in the disorganized store: anxiety, irritation, and perhaps even anger. The disorganization of the store contributes to these feelings. If the items had been organized more carefully and thoughtfully, the shopping experience would probably be far more successful and shoppers would feel calmer and happier. Certainly anxiety, irritation, and anger are not what we wish the children in our learning environment to feel. When materials for learning, such as blocks or paint, paper, and brushes, are stored and organized in thoughtful ways, it gives the message that these are important tools for learning. It also shows that the children are important because they are able to use the learning materials to their best advantage. In doing so, they feel far more positive about their learning experience than if they are trying to explore important ideas amidst disorganized chaos. Unlike the shoppers who need to search through a pile of items for an hour, the children are able to find what they need quickly and efficiently. It provides more time for learning and for conversations about learning.

By thinking seriously and carefully about your learning environment, you give a message to the children and their families that you care enough about them to plan and organize their environment to most effectively support learning. Let's take a closer look at the following considerations for planning an environment that nurtures conversations for learning:

- furnishings
- color and texture
- room arrangement
- material choice
- organization of materials
- sense of identity

Furnishings

The furnishings in an early childhood learning environment need to suit young children. They need to be of a size and height that will be comfortable for them. Children will not be able to fully focus and participate in a conversation while sitting at tables and chairs made for adults, because they will be uncomfortable and will not be able to see each other properly. Tables that hold four to six children are more encouraging and supportive to conversation than large, long tables or benches where children are too far away from each other to properly converse. Teachers can encourage conversation in outdoor areas by providing a picnic table and chairs or small park benches in quiet, shady places that invite two or three children to sit and talk. Indoor furniture that is light enough for teachers to easily move can be relocated outdoors temporarily to set the stage for a special conversation space.

It is also important to think about furnishings that invite children's families to engage in conversation with their children. A bench or sofa in a hallway or near the entrance to your room provides a place for adults to sit comfortably with their children, snuggling up close or holding them on their knee while chatting about the day.

Rebecca Marshall, principal of PS 347, feels so strongly about the importance of social and language learning during mealtimes that she changed the environment of the large school cafeteria. This windowless room was in the basement of the school, and children sat at long tables that had attached bench seating. The benches made it difficult for the students to get in and out of their seats, and made it hard to talk with other students. It was impossible for children with wheelchairs to fully participate in mealtime conversations or feel part of the community by sitting comfortably with their friends. Rebecca and a team of staff members and students selected new furniture: smaller round tables and chairs for six or so children. A small vase with a single flower was placed at the center of each table. The new environment resulted in amazing changes in the children's behavior. Children now talk more with the others at their table; they take greater care of the furniture and general meal environment; and the tone of the cafeteria has changed from chaotic to informal and relaxed.

In many early childhood learning environments, teachers use self-serve snack, where the children choose when to snack during their play and work time. This is a very effective way of creating longer uninterrupted playtime for children, but isn't always conducive to conversation. This is not so bad if the children also stay for a meal, say lunch or dinner, where they can talk with each other. But if snack is the only meal the children share together, you might consider how to make this time more nurturing to conversation. You don't necessarily need to change self-serve snack to family-style meals, but you can set the food and drink on a small table with chairs so small groups of children can sit together and talk while they snack. If children get snacks from their own bags, you can teach them to sit at a particular snack table or on a snack rug so they can talk with their friends. Simply laying a rug on the floor or under a tree creates a special place for snack, a special place for children to talk with each other, like being on a picnic together.

Many early childhood teachers use transportable shelving units in their rooms to create divisions between the block area, the dramatic play area, and the meeting area. The divisions create spaces with a clear purpose. Using shelving units to section off areas also avoids the creation of "runways" for children, and encourages children to work and talk within an area. Use shelving or display units low enough to allow a clear line of vision, so you can always see children at work and play from different parts of the room.

Color and Texture

Color and texture also play a role in establishing a tone within your environment. Certain colors create a sense of calm, and others can energize or excite. Can you imagine having your tooth drilled in a room painted iridescent orange or red? It would make you want to scream even before you heard the drill. Using softer hues and colors rather than traditional bright primary colors creates a quieter backdrop for learning in an early childhood setting. The children and their artwork then create the color and vibrancy for the room. Let the kind of activities that a space has been created for guide your choice of color for that area. If it is an area where children will be asked to listen to each other, such as the meeting or circle area, keep the shades muted rather than bright. It is easier to give attention to others when the surrounding visual noise is quiet. A mood of calm and security is best for conversations, and softer colors and textures can help achieve this.

If you can't change the color of your walls or carpet, consider instead the things you can change. For example, can you make your bulletin boards less visually noisy by backing them in softer hues rather than primary colors? Inexpensive brown, black, or white paper; cork; or wallpaper seconds work effectively. Can you display children's paintings on a wall with a color border that ties the paintings together visually and covers some of the bright wall color? Sometimes printing black-and-white photographs of children rather than always using color can attract more attention because of the contrast.

Teachers often ask children to sit on the floor or ground without considering how it might feel. The texture of the rug might be scratchy, or the floor cold and hard, but the children are asked to sit on it anyway. First ask if you would be comfortable sitting there before asking children to do so. When children gather together for conversation, they need to feel comfortable in order to give their attention as listeners and speakers. It is difficult to participate fully when sitting on a hard-paved outdoor area, a dirty carpet, or a scratchy rug. Take a critical look at the areas you use to gather children together for conversations. Would you like to sit on that texture for any amount of time? *Do* you sit there with the children? Consider whether there is another area where you can hold a given activity. Instead of children sitting on the pavement outside for lunch, can you put a picnic blanket under a tree so they are more comfortable? Rather than sitting on the hard floor, can you add a rug or move the children's small chairs to the area? If you are unable to change the flooring or texture, consider using small carpet squares or cushions. Some carpet stores donate their off-cuts, or families are often happy to wash cushion covers regularly, knowing they are helping their children have a comfortable place to sit while learning with each other.

Room Arrangement

The arrangement of furniture creates spaces within a learning environment. Each space fulfils a particular role and is there for a particular purpose. Sometimes these specific spaces are called centers or learning stations for small-group learning. Start by visualizing what will happen in each area during a busy school day. Imagine how many children will work there, what kinds of activities they will do, what materials they will use, and how this might change at different times of the day. Where do you visualize children gathering for whole-group meetings? Where do you imagine children working in small groups or pairs, perhaps in a studio space, drawing center, dramatic play area, or puppet center? Where will children use blocks, puzzles, paints, the water table, and so on?

Once you establish the purpose (or multiple purposes) for each area of your room, it is easier to see how much space is needed, the access children need to easily move in and out of the space, and the potential noise levels in each space. For example, you may decide the large area toward the rear of your room will be ideal for children to work in small groups using large blocks. Now that you know the purpose of the area, you can determine how much space you need for the shelves to hold the blocks, the space children need to move in and out of the area, and the amount of space three or four children need to build with blocks. Because you know that block play is often a noisy affair, you also determine that you would not put the writing and drawing table near the blocks because you want to promote that as a quieter, more private area for conversation between two or three children.

It is important, when thinking about space in terms of conversations, to give consideration to spaces where the whole group can talk, where small groups can gather and talk, and where one-to-one conversations can occur. The following section looks specifically at each of these spaces for conversation.

WHOLE-GROUP CONVERSATION SPACE

Whole-group conversations require space where a large number of children and the adults who work with them can meet in a circle. It is important to have enough space to form a circle because this promotes a more natural conversational setting where children can talk to each other and not just to the teacher. In a circle, children are able to make eye contact with each other, which encourages more child-to-child interaction. When sitting in a group in front of a teacher, it is very difficult for a child to make eye contact with a classmate who is sitting behind her. Sitting in a circle enables social skills to be learned and practiced, such as facing the speaker, using nonverbal cues, and taking turns. It is important to think about the best position in your room for this whole-group conversation space. It is usually best to locate this area away from the doorway or a noisy neighboring room so that the children's talk is supported by a quiet and peaceful environment, free from interruption.

Some early childhood settings are fortunate enough to have an outdoor space large enough for a whole-group conversation. An amphitheater-type space with benches or a ledge in a circular shape and shade overhead creates an outdoor space for large-group conversations. You could also create temporary whole-group space by laying picnic blankets on a grassy spot outside.

SMALL-GROUP CONVERSATION SPACE

Creating spaces where small groups can talk is essential both for spontaneous and planned conversations. Sometimes it's necessary for teachers to facilitate a conversation with a small group to delve deeper into a particular topic, so when creating these spaces in your learning environment, remember to make enough space for an adult to fit as well as the children. Spaces that allow four to six children to sit in a circle will encourage a more dynamic and natural communication path. You might call a small group to sit in a smaller version of the whole-group meeting space, particularly if you wish to be part of the conversation and facilitate the discussion. Alternatively, you might have space to ask a small group to sit around a small table, with a chair also for you. This can be a good place for documenting children's language because you can use the table to stabilize your writing. Flexible arrangements work best. In reality, most early learning settings do not have enough area to establish a separate small-group conversation space, but you can use other learning spaces for facilitated conversations too.

Remember to think about what is happening in the rest of the room and aim to gather your small conversation group in an area separate from noisy activities. For example, when other children are playing in the dramatic play and block areas, you could hold your facilitated conversation at the other side of the room, perhaps in an area where the children sit away from other children and do not have the visual distraction of the other children at play.

Also look closely at your outdoor space. Are there places where you can gather a small group at a picnic table or on a blanket? You can set up a small table and chairs under a tree and away from noisy play areas such as the sand pit.

The most enlightening conversations can often be those spontaneous conversations mentioned in chapter 1. Create spaces in your educational setting where children can work together, and they will usually talk also. Simply grouping tables together rather than setting them in single rows promotes collaborative work and conversation. Look for spaces in your class that provide children with talk and work space and provide you with a place to observe without taking an active role in the conversation. For example, there might be space for two children to paint side by side on two easels, and a space a little removed—perhaps behind the children or to the side of them—close enough to listen to the conversation without leading or changing it with your input.

ONE-TO-ONE CONVERSATION SPACE

Similar to the small-group settings, creating spaces for one-to-one conversation can create additional opportunities for talk. These spaces are more intimate, more private, and special. They are essential when the conversation topic is of a personal or private matter. The sensitive educator respects that children, no matter how young, have as much right to privacy as adults.

Recently I invited my young friends Nicholas and Charlie to spend some time at my home. I set up my old coffee table as a small drawing table where the boys could sit either side by side or facing each other. I placed a small container of black markers, another of crayons, and two pieces of drawing paper on the table. The boys chose to sit side by side, perched on soft cushions. I sat nearby, watching and listening with intrigue. The boys seemed to understand that I had set this space up just for them and that in itself created a specialness for them. I listened with delight as they chatted the afternoon away, discussing their ideas for drawings, helping each other draw different things, and showing a genuine interest in each other by their questions. The physical space and the shared act of drawing bound them together in conversation.

Where can you create an intimate space around an experience or material for the children? Perhaps you have a large beanbag chair or cushions that can be placed in a corner or in a quiet reading area, providing a soft and squishy place for two children to chat. A small coffee table can create intimacy in an area where two children can sit close to the ground rather than on chairs. Can you add a small park bench or log outdoors in a quiet place to encourage one-to-one conversation?

Taking Ownership

Draw a floor plan of your learning area, including the outdoor area. Using the numbers in the following list, mark each area of your floor plan with the type(s) of conversation that occur there.

1. whole-class conversations
2. small-group conversations
3. one-to-one conversations
4. children in conversation while working with others

Material Choice

The materials added to a space transform it and give it an identity. The materials you choose for an area can promote conversations for learning and influence the type of talk that occurs there. Materials in an imaginative play area during the beginning of the year, for example, could be props from the home (such as cooking utensils, recipe books, aprons, and baby dolls). The play conversations in this area will probably be about cooking, shopping, and caring for babies. Later in the year, the materials could be changed to include a cash register, menus, trays, and notepads. Conversations in this area will change in response to the new materials. They are now more likely to be about ordering and eating in a restaurant. These materials promote conversation because the roles children take on during their play relate to each other, and authentically interact.

In order to create an intimate space for one-to-one conversations, teachers Dave and Peggy placed a small round table in a corner of their room. They then used a ring to hang mosquito netting from the ceiling around the table. To the children, the lightweight fabric fell from the sky, encircling their special private table, creating a magical and secret place to be with a friend. The teachers did not enter this space, but kept it as a private space for two children to be together. The mosquito netting transformed this space, making it special and important.

Similarly, the materials you choose for mealtimes, either indoors or outdoors, create a tone for conversation. Setting the table with flowers, a small plant, a tablecloth, or placemats conveys the message that mealtimes are an important part of the day. It also shows children they are important because they are worth the trouble of making their meal space special. Soft music in the background, not loud enough to drown voices, can create a mood of relaxation and calm. These materials promote conversation because children will see mealtimes as important. They will be drawn to sit at the tables and talk with their friends.

Organization of Materials

The way you organize materials and displays can either enrich or clutter a conversation and learning space. Cluttered shelves filled with an assortment of containers, puzzles, games, and papers not only create visual noise, they make it harder for children to use materials effectively. Take a close look at your shelves. Are they cluttered like the shelves and clothes racks in the department-store story at the beginning of this chapter? Do they make you want to turn away, or do they invite you to stay awhile and choose a puzzle or just the right color crayon? Sometimes the shelves of early learning settings are so crowded I can't tell what materials are supposed to belong where. The children don't seem to know either. Nor do they see the importance of looking after the materials and returning them carefully to the place where they found them. The actual containers hold too many items to be used effectively and treated as a valuable learning tool.

Ellen Manobla, Marilla Baturay, Ned Brand, and I researched the effect of cluttered materials on children's interactions. We discovered that children were better able to take great care with materials, spend longer times with materials, and make more considered choices about materials (and therefore spend longer times engaged in their learning task) when the materials were organized in clear and uncluttered ways. It follows that if children spend more time at their learning task, they will spend more time in conversation about their learning. When they are frustrated at not being able to locate the marker, paper, or particular thread they wish to use, their conversation will instead be demanding, upsetting, or even aggressive.

This discovery led the teachers (Ellen, Marilla, and Ned) to:

- reduce how many containers they had on each shelf
- reduce how many materials were in each container
- store some materials away from learning spaces and "refresh" spaces during the year
- organize markers, crayons, and pencils in smaller containers and by color

Perhaps some of the behavior challenges teachers face with young learners can be avoided if more care is given to organizing their environment and learning materials. It is the teachers' responsibility to facilitate children's learning, and part of this means making the materials easy and efficient for the children to use, thereby avoiding conversations based on frustration and nurturing conversations based on choice, decision making, and learning.

Sense of Identity

Physical environment plays a powerful role in creating a sense of identity and belonging for each child. The first thing I look for when visiting a new early learning environment is a sense of identity. As I walk into the room, I ask myself, "Do I know who lives in this room? What is important in this room?" If I see children's paintings, drawings, or writing displayed, I know that children's learning is important to this teacher. When I see only store-bought charts on the walls, I get the message that the room belongs more to the teacher than to the children.

Each child needs to feel they have a place in your room. They need to see their image displayed and that their learning and play is valued and reflected in the environment. Even the way children's work is displayed gives a message to them and to visitors. Is it carefully backed with cardstock or construction paper to frame it and give it significance? Has care been taken to hang the work evenly and with a sense of order so the eye can appreciate each piece individually and as a whole? Or is the work randomly arranged on a bulletin board, with frayed edges and half hanging off the wall? Extreme examples, perhaps, but responsive teachers show the children that their work is valued by carefully and thoughtfully displaying it. Think of children's drawings or writing as a piece of art you wish to hang in your living room, and display it with the care it deserves.

The first thing I see when I enter Lauren and Gary's first-grade classroom is a small bookcase facing the doorway. Plants on the top shelf bring softness and life into the old school building. On the shelves are simple wooden picture frames, bought at the dollar store across the street, containing delightful photographs of each child. There is no doubt what—or who—is important in this room. In Cheritha and Dax's first-grade classroom, each child has a special place for reading time and a special bin for their own things, clearly labeled with the child's name and photograph. The children know they belong to the class because they have these places that belong just to them.

It is also important for families to see their identity in your learning space. For the child to feel she belongs, her family must also belong. Teachers Debra, Zaphira, and Elsa take photographs of their children with the family member who brings them to school each day. These are displayed in small wooden frames. Each day, the children and their families are greeted by their own image as they enter the room, telling them that this is *their* space and they belong here.

You can also ask each family to share an item of significance with you and the children, and to allow you to keep it in your learning environment for a while. Display these items with pride and care. This is a particularly powerful strategy for helping families come together as one group, learn about each other, and feel their unique identities are respected and valued. Ask each family personally, with their child present, so they understand your interest in their family. If families do not have a particular artifact they could lend you, ask if they would help you choose an appropriate photograph from the Internet or a library book. Display each item with a context statement that explains why it is important to your room.

When children and families see their identity reflected in the learning environment, they feel a sense of belonging. The shared images of self bind people together in a community. They say "We belong here and we all belong together." This is the foundation for building relationships with children and their families, and for engaging in conversation with them.

Taking Ownership

How will you ensure that the children and their families have a strong sense of identity in your setting? Review the ideas in the previous passages. Make a list of possibilities for you and your context. Don't limit the ideas; write as many as you can. Then circle the two ways you believe are achievable and manageable for you to implement. Act on them.

How does your environment show that you also belong to the learning group? How is your identity reflected? For example, are there photographs of you and your family alongside the children's families? Do you also share a favorite book from home in the library display shelves?

Structuring the Day for Conversation

The bottom line of scheduling is there are only so many hours in a day. Teachers today struggle with an overcrowded curriculum, and each day there seems to be a new curriculum or a new program that early learning settings are asked to embrace. In order to cope with these ever-increasing pressures, teachers need to make wise and thoughtful decisions as to what to do and what not to do. A clear and well-articulated vision will help you make these choices.

By reading this book, you have already shown your interest in children learning from and with each other. You are interested in creating a climate of risk-free learning by listening to the children and learning from their conversations.

Like most adults, I'm sure you can recall a day when you felt rushed and pushed for time. On such days, there is too much to do and not enough hours in the day to do it all. You end up feeling hurried, tired, and stressed. As adults, it might just be that we tried to do too much in one day, or didn't plan enough time for each task. Perhaps something unpredicted happened and took time away from the tasks you thought you would do.

It is not so different for young children. Sometimes their days feel rushed and stressful to them. However, the difference is that *they* are not the ones in control of making it rushed and stressful. Unconsciously, teachers often schedule children's days to be so full of different activities that there is little time for savoring and exploring each learning opportunity. The structure of your program needs to provide a rhythm for a young learner's day, but it does not need to be rigidly timed. It is more effective for learning to follow the natural rhythms of the children and their learning. This will help keep the children from feeling stressed and pushed through their day.

At the same time, it is important not to give up structure altogether because structure gives rhythm to your day. Think of the structure of your day like using a map to show the way to your destination (that is, to learning for the children). It is okay to take a detour from the planned route when you see something interesting. Be guided by the children, and sense when they need five minutes more to continue playing or to watch the new butterflies emerge from their chrysalis. Use your observations to decide when to stop a whole-group conversation and pick it up another day because the children are distracted. You might detour on some days, but remember you will always return to the original route and continue your journey for the day.

Sometimes teachers need to do what I refer to as a "spring-cleaning" of their schedules and curriculums. Are there times during the day or areas of your curriculum that are less than completely satisfying to you as a teacher or, more important, to the children as learners? Are the children performing some tasks more as busywork than engaged learning? Can you reimagine the learning environment in a way that will include more time and opportunity for talk? Your answers to these questions will help make more time for conversations during the busy school week. Let's look more closely at ways to ensure there is time during your day both for spontaneous and facilitated conversations.

Time for Spontaneous Conversations

Conversational moments happen throughout the day. Earlier (on pages 44–46), we explored the value of interacting with and listening to children's spontaneous conversations. These conversations, such as when a child excitedly greets you in the morning wearing her brand-new sneakers or when a child tells a story during snacktime of his new puppy who kept the family awake the night before, can be so much fun and offer great insight into children's interests and schema. Spontaneous conversations can occur at any time, as long as you give children time to talk. Think for a moment about the amount of time you plan for the following:

- arrival and departure
- snack- and mealtime
- uninterrupted play and exploration

Are you providing enough time for spontaneous conversation to flourish? Teachers can unconsciously value only the times they are in conversation with children by planning more time for teacher-directed experiences. However, children need many opportunities to engage in conversation with each other during the day.

ARRIVAL AND DEPARTURE

Arrival time can often be hectic and frantic when many children come in the door at once. Sometimes it feels like a jolt of change for a child, rather than a smooth transition and an opportunity for conversation. To help with this, create a window of time for arrival (fifteen minutes, for example) rather than one distinct time. It is important to clearly communicate this to families. Think about how different these two messages sound: "Arrive at school at 9:00 AM" and "Arrive at school between 8:45 and 9:00 AM." This window of time for arrival allows enough time to make the transition, talk with friends, connect with families, and talk with the teacher if needed.

Give some thought to how you can structure the environment and materials to ensure that arrival time is a smooth transition. How can you be near the door to greet each family without being drawn to supervise the others who have already arrived? Think about what you can set out for children to do with their families as they arrive. For example, you can set up table puzzles or playdough for children to work with, or put out books for children to read with their family members. Children will be able to talk with each other, families will have time to talk with other families, and you will have time to listen to all the exciting events that happened overnight or over the weekend. You can even play soft music as the children arrive, immediately creating a calm atmosphere and giving a message about the tone, noise, and behavior expected in your setting.

At the end of the day, rather than rushing children out the door, have them collect their bags and coats five minutes before dismissal. This gives children a little bit more time to chat with each other in a relaxed atmosphere. There won't be time for long conversations, of course, but a more relaxed pace will give you and the children more time for conversation other than just your directions and "hurry along." Another strategy is to dismiss the children but allow them to return to the room with their family. This gives them a few minutes to talk about the display of paintings or the photos from their recent field trip.

Teacher Stacy prints extra copies of photographs she has taken of children working during the day. She encourages families to collect these photographs at the end of the day and take them home. The photographs provide a link between home and school, and also provide something concrete for each child and family to talk about.

With smaller groups of children, or if families collect children at varying times, it is helpful to think of departure time as similar to arrival time. Teachers who think of the farewell time as ten minutes to talk with children and their families, rather than as a one- or two-minute "handover," approach the children and their families differently. These teachers know they need time to listen and talk. Departure time isn't just handing over a child to her family, but a transition from school to home, and there is often a lot to talk about to support this.

SNACK- AND MEALTIME

Snack- and mealtime are some of the most important learning times in a young child's day. Among other things, children learn social skills, new vocabulary, and fine-motor coordination. In order to value meals and snacks as times for spontaneous conversation, teachers need to schedule enough time for these activities. When you schedule more than a quick ten minutes for children to eat, you are giving them time to chat with their friends. Family-style mealtimes provide children and teachers the opportunity for spontaneous conversation with each other in small groups. Meals and snacks become times that mark the day as well as a time of rich learning.

UNINTERRUPTED PLAY AND EXPLORATION

Children need time to be with each other if they are going to be in conversation with each other. Valuing learning through conversation means valuing time when children talk with each other as much as the time when they talk with adults. Young children will learn and grow from spontaneous conversations during block play or imaginative play, while they sort and organize groups of different colored beads, as they explore volume and capacity at the water table, and so on.

However, too often this time is cut short. Meaningful conversations cannot happen in just a few minutes. It often takes children (and adults) some time to get into an experience. Teachers need to allow children time to *enter* the experience, and then more time to *be in* conversation and learning before calling for cleanup time.

The imaginative play area is a perfect example of this. You may have noticed that many times when a small group of children enter an imaginative play area, they spend the first five or so minutes moving materials around. They are getting to know the space and the materials. It's like a warm-up to play. It takes time to get into the play. Often children's play will begin as parallel play, with children playing side by side, not together in a common story. By providing longer uninterrupted time for play, you allow children more time to work through this stage and into the time when they begin to assign roles and make the decisions necessary for their play that day. This can often take longer than the actual playing out of a story. So much learning is happening through talk, but it can only happen if they are given time to do so.

Too often teachers either schedule short periods of play, or at a certain time *they* decide all children need to change areas. Put yourself in the shoes of the children who are just about to embark on an exciting adventure they have been working out with each other, and the teacher says they have to move centers. How would you feel? Young children need time to talk with each other about their play and explorations because these are meaningful things for them to talk about. Allowing children to make the decision about when to change play areas is more effective for conversation and learning. It shows children you respect them as competent thinkers and view them as capable of making sensible decisions. In order to create a culture of conversation in the learning environment, teachers must challenge themselves to provide this time, and notice when they might unconsciously be cutting it short.

Time for Facilitated Conversations

It is important to provide time for facilitated conversations during your day. Facilitated conversations offer you the opportunity to delve deeper into children's ideas by initiating a topic for conversation. Facilitated conversations occur within whole-group meetings, in small groups, or during one-to-one conversations.

Class meetings, such as the morning meeting or regular whole-group conversations (for example, the before and after Investigation Time meetings Dawn and Vanessa held with their kindergartners), provide a regular time each day to facilitate conversation and delve more deeply into children's thinking. Ten to fifteen minutes at the beginning of a session may seem like a lot of time, particularly if you have a half-day program, but when used for purposeful conversation, this time provides you with much insight into children's emerging theories, and provides children with valuable learning opportunities. You may not need the same amount of time for the beginning meeting each day. If you are having difficulty making time for this whole-group meeting, you could try gathering the children together every day, but facilitate a conversation only three out of five days. On the other days, you could still hold a class meeting but not spend as much time together in conversation.

When children arrive and leave at different times, the beginning of the session might not be the best time to facilitate a whole-group conversation. It might be more effective to facilitate more small-group conversations, during which you can follow the interests and ideas of three or four children. However, when children share the same learning space, it is important to find times to gather them all together at some stage so they have a sense of community with each other. Look for times during your day when this might be possible, such as before center time, after story time, or after snack.

Many small-group and one-to-one conversations can be facilitated while other children are engaged in learning areas or centers. Coteachers should work together to ensure that one teacher supervises the children playing while the other teacher is facilitating a small-group conversation. If you do not have a coteacher, try facilitating small-group conversations when a family member or two are able to be in the room with you to help with supervision. Or choose a time when the other children are engaged in a favorite activity. For example, in a home-care situation, while some children are immersed playing with playdough or pretending they are at a grocery store, you can facilitate a conversation with two or three other children. You can supervise the busy group while in the same general area, and at the same time talk with two or three others. Remember, these conversations do not have to be long in duration. Just three to five minutes of conversation has the potential to reveal children's thinking to you.

Although mealtimes are a great opportunity for spontaneous conversation, they also provide the chance for you to facilitate a conversation. You might find this time particularly useful if you care for a small group of children in your home. It might be one of the few times you have all the children awake and together at the same time. You can also initiate a conversation with a small group after you have read them a book, as they sit on your lap and either side of you. You have the children close to you, and you also have a shared experience to talk about.

Finally, it is sometimes easier to make time to facilitate a conversation with one child or a small group while they are engaged in learning. For example, you might have noticed that Joe and Harrison like to play with the toy trains every day. You decide to discover more about their prior knowledge of trains, and so you sit with them while they are playing, listening to their conversation and gently asking questions. While this is not as formal as a whole-group or small-group meeting, you are still engaged in conversation for a particular purpose, and you ask questions to explore ideas about the given topic more deeply. Alternatively, you can introduce an item, such as a model of a train tunnel or a photograph of a steam engine, and take this to where the boys are playing. You have taken the conversation to the boys rather than removing them from their play to have a conversation. Just be careful not to do this too often. Children need time just for playing too.

Taking Ownership

Are there times in your day with young children when you feel rushed or pushed for time? Chances are, the children feel the same way during these times. What can you do to change this? Are you trying to do too much during this time? Can you "spring-clean" and remove some tasks, or move them to another time of day, to provide more time for uninterrupted play and conversation?

Sometimes it is difficult to honestly and realistically view a situation when intimately involved in it. Step outside your regular day to take a critical look at your arrival, departure, transition, or mealtimes. Ask a coteacher to lead or supervise this time so you can step back and observe. Or set up a video camera on a tripod to record this time for ten minutes. What do you notice about the pace and flow? Do children have time to talk? Is the tone hectic and noisy or smooth and calm? Whose voice is heard the most? Do you need to make any changes?

A Climate for Conversation

A learning environment is more than the physical layout and arrangement of the room. It includes the emotional climate also. The emotional climate is how you feel when you enter a room and how you feel while you are within a room. For optimal learning and conversation, you will want to create an emotional climate in which each person feels safe and secure, takes risks, tries new things, and therefore learns.

What kind of an environment supports young learners to confidently and openly participate in conversations? An environment that tells children and their families that they belong there; a space that communicates that it is *theirs:* a shared space. Children and their families feel they belong there together in relationship with each other. This kind of setting is a place children want to be, and where they feel confident to be themselves, to take risks, and to participate fully. An environment like this will support relationships of trust and respect. Such an environment is created when teachers make time to get to know the children and their families, and create consistency and predictability for young learners.

Learn About the Children and Their Families

To be in relationships of mutual trust and respect, you need to know who you are in relationship with. To know a child is to also know her family. The two cannot be separated in a teacher's thinking. The first thing to do is to consciously and intently *listen* to the child and her family. Teachers sometimes forget to do this first. Such a deceptively simple thing, but listening first is a gift to the other person. It shows the child she is important to you. Your genuine interest in her will convey powerful messages about her value, and will establish a relationship of respect and trust. The more you listen, the more you will learn. And most of the time, the more the child and her family will share and participate in conversation with you. Other specific strategies to learn about the children and their families include:

- Get-to-Know-You Chats

  At the beginning of the year, schedule ten-minute get-to-know-you chats with each child and family. Focus this time on *listening to* the family members, not telling them about your program or philosophy. Ask them to tell you about their child at home: what she likes to do, what they like to do together, and so on. Keep the conversation informal and welcoming. It is amazing how powerful it can be to know the names of a child's family members, that she has a pet kitten called Fluffy, and that her grandmother lives next door.

- Meet-the-Teacher Events

  In a similar way, many teachers hold a Meet the Teacher evening or morning during which an informal setting—such as coffee and cookies in the morning, a potluck dinner, or a picnic in the park—allows relationships between home and school to develop. This communicates important messages to children: they are important, their family is important, and also that their family sees the teacher and school as important.

- One-to-One or Small-Group Conversations

  Ensure you spend some quality one-to-one or small-group time with each child, particularly during the beginning weeks of the year. Make a list in your planning book and check off when you are able to do this with each child so as not to accidentally leave a child out. This conversation could take place during a few moments of playing blocks together, while reading a book snuggled up on the library cushions, or while sitting with a different group of students during snack or breakfast each day.

- Individual Notes

  Carry a small notebook with you in a pocket or place one near your space for talking so you can quickly make notes of what the children talk about with you. This will help you quickly build knowledge of each child's individual interests and things that are important to them.

- Unique Characteristics

  Set a goal for yourself to learn one unusual or interesting thing about each child within the first two weeks of school. You can learn about children by watching them play or listening to conversations, or in a more structured way by scheduling a special day for each child when they bring in something they love to share with the group. Make a special display table for these treasured objects. Share about yourself too.

- Summer Mementos

  Teachers Kathie, Carol, and Ferdinand often begin their prekindergarten year by asking children to bring a summer memento to school. The teachers and the children share through a movie ticket, a shell, a sun hat from Florida, or a drawing of their bike. The children's (and teachers') stories are told, typed, and displayed with pride alongside their mementos.

Taking Ownership

Write down the name of each child. Next to each name, write something you know about that child, such as the child's interests, names of pets, favorite food, what he or she likes to do at home, and so on. Challenge yourself to name things that have not been directly observed in your learning environment. Can you do this for each child? Are there children you need to spend more time with so you know them better?

How will you get to know all of the young learners and their families? Make a list of possibilities for you and your context. Don't limit the ideas; write as many as you can. Then circle the two ways you believe are achievable and manageable for you to implement. Act on them.

Create Consistency and Predictability

Learning is an emotional as well as a cognitive experience. Children feel that it is safe to participate when a climate of trust and security has been established. The strong routines you teach and practice at the beginning of the year will provide a predictable environment. When children know what to do, have support to become independent, and are not expected to do it automatically, they feel secure. Children benefit from having predictable routines. When they know what to expect from their day, it is much easier for them to fully participate without uncertainty. Aim to keep consistency in your day without becoming rigid. There is no need to watch the clock and time your day to precision. It is better to follow the timing of the children and pace your day according to how they are interacting and participating.

You can create consistency and predictability when you gather children together for a morning meeting in the same way each day, or by using the same signal and transition for cleaning up after center time. Another example of consistency is having children choose a book from the shelf and read on the rug area each time your group changes activities. You might use a routine or ritual for mealtime such as having children help you put out cups, or begin every afternoon naptime by playing soft music and holding a child in your lap as you read to her. Your morning routine might include starting the children off with playdough, which gives you time for greeting and welcoming other children and families. The children soon learn these routines and use them to mark their day. It gives their day a rhythm, and the predictability allows them to relax and fully participate.

Many teachers use a predictable structure for their morning meeting because they see the benefit for the children of beginning each day in a familiar way. For example, the meeting might begin with a greeting game or song followed by the teacher reading a message or letter she has written to the children. The letter (often called a morning message) tells the children about the day, and is another way to create predictability and consistency.

Finally, to truly provide consistency and predictability for young learners, teachers need to keep their word. This may sound obvious, but if you tell a child you will do something, you need to follow through and do it. If a child misses her turn in a game and the teacher says, "It can be your turn first tomorrow," the teacher needs to make sure it *is* her turn first tomorrow, writing her name on a reminder note so as not to forget, if needed. Put yourself in the shoes of the four-year-old who sees this kind of passing comment as a promise, and then learns the teacher did not keep the promise. Similarly, it is important not to threaten children with actions you will not or cannot follow through with. When teachers make threats such as "If you do that again, I'll call Mommy," or "Because you drew on the table, you're not allowed to use the crayons again," and don't have any intention of calling Mommy or removing the child from the crayons forever, children learn not to trust the word of their teachers.

Taking Ownership

How do you create a predictable and safe environment for learning? Reflect on your current schedule and think about transition times. What is your current routine for these transitions? Is the routine different for each transition? Is there a consistent strategy you can use to let children know it is time to transition, time to clean up, and so on?

What can the children count on each day? Make a list of all the things that are predictable for them. How does this structure or routine support their sense of security? Does it provide opportunities to be flexible when needed?

Conclusion

The educators in Reggio Emilia talk of the environment as another teacher for children (Gandini 1998). This idea provides us with a powerful way to think about the impact of environment on learning. It can help or hinder us in the learning and teaching process. We are all affected by the environment we find ourselves in. It affects our mood, our emotions, and our ability to participate. Learning environments need to be places of learning, joy, and hope. They are places where people are in relationship with each other, and therefore need to be places of interaction and talk.

There are many excellent resources that more fully explore the powerful role environment plays in learning. To learn more you can read books such as *Designs for Living and Learning* by Deb Curtis and Margie Carter, *Child Care Design Guide* by Anita Rui Olds, and *Caring Spaces, Learning Places* by Jim Greenman.

You might not be able to implement all the ideas in this chapter. In fact, that would be impossible for just one program to do. Choose those that are right for you and the children in your care. Try some new ideas and give yourself time to become familiar with your new ways. Each program and every group of children are different, so modify these strategies so they work for you.

References

Curtis, D., and M. Carter. 2003. *Designs for Living and Learning.* St. Paul: Redleaf Press.

Gandini, L. 1998. "Educational and Caring Spaces." In *The Hundred Languages of Children,* ed. C. Edwards, L. Gandini, and G. Forman. Greenwich, Conn.: Ablex Publishing.

Greenman, J. 2005. *Caring Spaces, Learning Places: Children's Environments that Work.* Redmond, Wash.: Exchange Press.

Rui Olds, A. 2001. *Child Care Design Guide.* New York: McGraw-Hill.

CHAPTER FOUR

Facilitating Conversations

"Good teachers are the ones you can ask questions to and you don't feel stupid if you do."
—Sam, six years old

"She listens to us, like when we have a class meeting about something important. She asks us what we think."
—Daniel, seven years old

We have explored the importance of creating a learning environment that provides the conditions for conversations and that allows teachers to use conversations as a window into the thinking of young children. We have also explored how teachers' beliefs about children, intelligence, and learning influence how they interact with their young learners, and our role in creating the best environment to nurture conversation. This chapter explores the teacher's role more deeply by looking at ways teachers facilitate conversations that enrich and challenge the growth of children's young minds. This chapter offers some strategies for effectively talking with young children.

> *"It's surprising how little most three- and four-year-olds value their own words when they come into our classrooms. Once they've been with us for a while, they begin to realize on a very deep level how much their words are valued as a reflection of who they are. This is our program's legacy to them now and forever—they will always feel they have something worthwhile to say."*
>
> —Zaphira Azoulay, teacher of three- and four-year-olds

Learning specific strategies for facilitating conversations will help you get in touch with children's thinking. To do this, teachers need to learn the following skills:

- listening carefully
- embracing silence
- asking good questions
- helping children develop conversational skills
- summarizing conversations
- using memory tools
- bringing conversations to a close

Listening Carefully

It seems to be stating the obvious that a book about children's conversation will have a section about listening. However, so many resources about children's language tend to focus on teaching children how to be good listeners. While listening effectively is an essential skill for learning and for life, it is also important for *teachers* to listen effectively to children. By listening to children, you will be able to plan a curriculum with the children clearly in mind. Listening carefully means:

- listening with intent
- listening to children's thinking
- giving up control of conversations
- honoring children's ideas
- beginning small

Listening with Intent

The phrase "listening with intent" emphasizes the difference between listening and merely hearing. Teachers often hear the voices of children. They hear their words and make sense of them in a superficial way. This is hearing without listening. To get to children's thinking, you need to listen beyond their words and listen to their ideas. You need to be in the moment, both in body and mind. It is easy to look like an attentive listener: sitting still, body leaning forward toward the speaker, making eye contact, and occasionally nodding your head. But how many times have you found yourself wandering off in thought during these times? I do it more often than I'd like to admit. It is natural after hearing an idea for our thinking to be sent off on a tangent, but the more you are aware of this happening, the better able you are to redirect your attention back to what the speaker is saying.

Listening to Children's Thinking

Listening to young children's thinking rather than just hearing their words is not always easy, particularly in a busy and noisy learning environment. In fact, it is not easy to do in any environment, including adult environments. When a person is talking while her ideas are being created, or "thinking aloud," these ideas are often communicated in a haphazard way. I always cringe when listening to voice recordings of myself in planning meetings or conference presentations because to my critical ear I sound inarticulate, and the ideas I'm trying to communicate are not always fully formed. My language is definitely not always grammatically correct, but the ideas seem to get through anyway.

The first step in effectively listening to children's thinking is to take time. It sometimes takes a lot of time and patience to make sense of what children are telling you. Because you want to discover their thinking, their emerging theories, confusions, and ideas, it will be more challenging than listening to them tell you a series of facts, such as the colors in a rainbow or how many buttons are on their shirt. The strategies for collecting and interpreting conversations explored in later chapters will also help you develop skills in listening beyond the words. The more you practice listening to children, the more skilled you will become. The most important thing is to remember that you are listening for children's unique thinking about the world, not for them to regurgitate facts to you. Take time to be in the moment with children and to give them the time to form, create, and share ideas with you.

Giving Up Control of Conversations

In traditional teacher-student interactions the teacher remains in control of where the conversation will go. The teacher decides the topic; he decides the questions he will ask; and he decides which of the students will answer them. If the teacher doesn't like the answers given by the students, he will ask the question again, perhaps changing it slightly, until someone can give the answer he is seeking. Sometimes, he might give clues such as, "You're almost right" or "Not quite . . . it's something to do with what Jose said." I call this "guess what's in the teacher's head" questioning because the teacher is seeking one specific answer to his question. In such conversations, the teacher is always in control of the final destination for the conversation. He knows the outcome because he has planned for it and will ensure his questions lead to it.

To truly listen to another person, you must give away part of your personal control. This means the other speaker has the power to take the conversation to places unknown to you. You are no longer completely controlling the route or destination of the conversation. This is where many teachers feel unnerved or challenged in creating a culture of conversation.

Teacher education often focuses on training new teachers to ask questions that test children's knowledge of what has been taught, which is a very controlling type of conversation. Giving children control of conversations can be scary, so take it slowly. Gradually loosen your control of knowing where the conversation is going to go. Be open to where the children take it. The first step is to think about the purpose of your conversation, and then ask more questions that seek to uncover children's thinking, rather than questions that tell you the answer you already know. View it as an exciting mystery journey.

Honoring Children's Ideas

Some of the conversations you have each day should be for the purpose of uncovering children's thinking. There will still be times when it will be appropriate to have conversations that gain specific information from children (such as "Do you want pasta or chicken for lunch today?" or "Where do the scissors belong?"), but more and more, your conversations will be focused on uncovering children's thinking or their ideas about something. Instead of making assumptions about what they are thinking, what they know, or what they would like to do, begin to increasingly ask them for their opinions and ideas.

When the children in Ellen and Marilla's preschool class showed an interest in musical instruments, the teachers were not sure how to introduce these items to the dramatic play area in a meaningful way. "Let's take it to the children in a whole-group meeting," they decided. "I wonder what the children's ideas are?"

Ellen and Marilla asked the children, "How do you think we can play with musical instruments in the dramatic play area? What could the dramatic play area become so we can play with musical instruments?" After an animated discussion, the group decided it could become an instrument repair store. Three children agreed to work on creating the store environment that day. The instrument repair store—complete with sign, sheet music, instruments, and "bill paper"—sustained and enriched play conversations in the classroom for many weeks.

Slowly begin to use your conversations with children to uncover their ideas. Next time you read a book to a child or a group, rather than asking children to retell the storyline, ask them what they thought of the book. Ask questions such as "What did you think of that? What was the funniest/scariest/saddest part for you? Would you do the same thing as this character? What did you think when this happened?" Next time you want to set up materials for collage work, ask one or two children to help you to choose the materials that will be used. The next time there is an opportunity for children to construct something within a larger inquiry (creating a car from cardboard boxes within a study about cars, a castle within a study about fairytales, or a model of a butterfly within a study of spring, for example), ask the children to decide what materials they will need. Help them make a list of materials, and collect the materials over a few days. Facilitate conversations about the best materials for the activity. Explore new possibilities for using materials, talk about which part of the construction should be made first, and so on. Use these conversations to explore the children's ideas. Do not tell them the materials *you* think will work best, but allow them the learning experience of discovering this for themselves.

Beginning Small

As you become more consciously aware of listening with intent, it might help to start by sitting alongside a child or small group of children and just concentrate on being in the moment *with* them. Being in the moment means making the decision and then taking the action to give time to children. Do not go there with your own agenda. Do not go there seeking to find out something in particular. That will come later. Start with just being there, listening to their words and taking notice of what they are talking about. Participate if you are invited to, but otherwise, don't interrupt. It does not need to be for a substantial amount of time; begin with a minute or two of being present and listening. Starting with some moments like these each day will help you become attuned to the children and begin to listen first instead of talking first.

Listening may feel odd initially. Teachers are so used to being the main talker in their learning environment, and sometimes they subconsciously think if they're not talking, they're not teaching, and therefore the children aren't learning. Developing an understanding of learning through a social-constructivist view and of the child as capable help move you from this standpoint, but some habits are hard to break.

Make sure you choose a time that won't be interrupted. For example, don't choose to be in the moment with a small group just as other children are arriving in the morning or when lunch is delivered to your room. Wait for the rest of the group to be settled and engaged in other tasks, or choose a moment when there is an extra adult in the room who can supervise and help the rest of the children.

Choose the time and the place carefully so you won't be tempted by other competing demands. For example, instead of serving lunch at the sink area and then standing by the lunch tables to supervise, you might sit with one small group and listen to what they are talking about as they eat their lunch. Or you could sit near children playing in the sandbox and listen to their conversation without taking part in it.

In the beginning, try to listen for a minute or two at a time. The point is to spend even a little bit of time truly listening to what children are saying, rather than listening haphazardly and halfheartedly because of competing demands on your time. Gradually you will build on and expand this listening time by using some of the strategies explored later in this chapter.

Taking Ownership

Choose a time when you can be in the moment with a small group of children in conversation with each other. Choose a time when you will have little distraction and can give the children the gift of your time and attention. Read the section above for ideas.

Listen with intent to the children's conversation. That's all. Just listen.

The next day, return to the same area or the same group. Listen with intent again.

After listening to a few conversations like this, reflect on what you discovered. Did the children talk about different things? Were the conversations connected to the task or learning experience the children were involved in? Were there any common themes or ideas the children talked about across different days?

Embracing Silence

Adults are often afraid of silence in conversations. It takes time to reach a level of comfort with someone when moments of silence do not make us squirm. Some adults have a harder time than others and try to fill any gap in the conversation with chatter.

Teachers bring their own social understanding into a learning environment. When a child is silent during a conversation, teachers often make assumptions such as the child doesn't understand, he doesn't know, or he is refusing to answer. However, it might just mean the child is thinking about the teacher's question or about his ideas. Of course, it might mean he doesn't understand the question and the teacher needs to rephrase and ask it again. But if teachers always jump in without giving children time to think, they run the risk of making the wrong assumption.

There is no way to know exactly what is going on inside a child's mind. Waiting and allowing the silence to be present will help you honor the child's thinking process and ideas. You will often be rewarded with an unexpected response from the child, or even a response from a different child who can read the social cues and sees the silence as an opportunity to contribute to the conversation.

It is also important to value silence in terms of encouraging more child-to-child talk. The vast majority of conversations in learning environments tend to be led by the teacher and have question–answer–new question–new answer patterns. These conversations flow between adult and child and rarely between children themselves. They communicate many things to young children: that the teacher is in control of the conversation, that the most important talk is when children talk to the teacher, and that children can learn only from the teacher.

When creating a learning environment for young children to learn from each other, you need to purposefully aim for more child-to-child interactions and fewer teacher-dominated conversations. This can be particularly difficult when working with children whose previous school experience has taught them to talk in other ways. They may have already learned to value only the talking they do to the teacher. They need time, modeling, encouragement, and experience to learn how to talk with each other in a group conversation. They need time to learn how to respond to their classmates' ideas, and not just those of their teacher.

Chapter 3 explored how the arrangement of the conversation space, in terms of where the teacher and children sit, can influence child-to-child conversation. Allowing for silence in conversation helps children see that important conversations can be more than back-and-forth tennis matches with the teacher. A silence allows another child the opportunity to contribute, and breaks the cycle of teacher-child-teacher. You might simply look around the group, using body language in a way to suggest you are searching for more ideas from the group, or with a nod of your head and a smile suggest a child with something to say can go ahead.

Chapter 2 discussed how important it is to break the teacher-child-teacher cycle by providing thinking time, or, in a very subtle but powerful way, children will learn that the only important responses are those they make to the teacher. They learn they do not need to listen to their peers' ideas because they are never asked to think about or comment on them.

Asking Good Questions

Allowing the voice of children to be heard in a learning environment does not imply that the teacher takes an inactive role in conversations. Questioning is a critical part of your role in guiding conversations. When the purpose of a conversation is to uncover children's ideas, the "guess what's in the teacher's head" questions will not do. They will not allow you to achieve your purpose. They will not result in greater insight into children's true schema. "Guess what's in the teacher's head" questions merely confirm to children that the teacher's ideas are the "right" ones. Over time they learn to give responses that please the teacher, not responses that show their thinking.

Some questions will lead to more creative thought or open sharing than others. The most important starting point is to understand that the purpose of these questions is to uncover the children's ideas, not to reinforce the teacher's existing thinking or test children's knowledge. If you are very clear about this, you will find it easier to filter out questions that do not elicit broad answers and varying perspectives.

It is helpful to look more closely at the different kinds of questions in order to deepen your own understanding of the questions you most regularly use. The next section will look briefly at the following types of questions:

- open-ended questions
- questions that delve deeper into children's thinking
- questions that clarify and focus ideas
- questions that connect experiences or ideas

Open-ended Questions

Open-ended questions were discussed in chapter 2. When I was in college, open-ended questions were called "fat" questions, and closed questions were called "skinny" questions. What a great mental image these terms create. Fat questions create an image of expanse, sumptuousness, and abundance. Skinny questions create an image of frugality or constraint.

Open-ended (fat) questions are more likely to receive a long answer or multiple answers. They have the possibility of richness in perspective and ideas. They are "owned" by the person giving the answer because the question does not seek a definitive, one-right answer.

Closed (skinny) questions have only one right answer. "Guess what's in the teacher's head" questions exemplify this because the teacher already knows the answer he's looking for. Closed questions often block different perspectives or alternative ideas to those of the questioner. The answer is "owned" by the questioner, not necessarily by the person giving the response.

EXAMPLES OF CLOSED AND OPEN-ENDED QUESTIONS

CLOSED	OPEN-ENDED
What are you making?	Tell me about this.
	How did you do that?
Does the light come from the sun?	Where can we see light?
	How do we get light?
Is the school building tall or short?	What do you notice about the school building?
	What do you see when you look at the building next door?
	What do you see when you look up/down?
Did you put the block there to stop it from falling over?	Why did you put the block there?
	What happened when you put the block there?
	What do you want the block to do?
Do you think we could see if we had no windows?	Why do we have windows?
	What do windows do?
	What would it be like with no windows?

It is important to understand how open-ended and closed questions create or limit possibilities and multiple ideas. Then you can see how important it is to pay attention to asking more open-ended questions when your goal is to uncover children's thinking.

Closed questions can lead children to a particular idea and, in doing so, lead them away from their own original thoughts. It is important for teachers to be aware of how they may unwittingly lead children to think the way they do, or unknowingly lead one child to connect to an idea from another child when it might not have the same meaning for both children. Teachers sometimes put words into children's mouths when they expect children to think in their adult terms.

For example, during the following conversation with four-year-old Alice, I made an assumption based on my own schema, and it did not match hers.

Alice:	My brain's a balloon.
Lisa (adult):	A balloon?
Alice:	Yep, a big balloon. [giggling]
Lisa:	So it gets bigger like a balloon does? How interesting. How does the brain get bigger?
Alice:	*No . . . it's round* like a balloon. See? [shows me her drawing]

Alice had the confidence to tell me my understanding was incorrect, but it made me wonder how often I do the same thing to other children I teach. Perhaps they don't have Alice's confidence to tell me I don't understand. I can now see how my question "So it gets bigger like a balloon does?" led Alice in a particular direction, which in this case was not the direction she was headed. It is a closed question—she could answer yes or no—but it is also a leading question. It led her to *my* understanding, *my* idea, *my* schema about the brain and balloons; not her idea.

This brief conversation with Alice alerted me to be more careful about assuming I know what children mean by their metaphors and language. By remaining clear that your purpose is to uncover children's thinking, to be a researcher of their mind's workings, you are more likely to be alert to questions that might lead children in a less than meaningful direction for them.

Questions That Delve Deeper into Children's Thinking

Some questions are open and specifically seek to get more detail or more information. They are like a mini bulldozer, gently digging at the ground to uncover the layers beneath the topsoil. These are the most helpful kinds of questions when you want to understand children's thinking. Delving questions search for more information. If I could rewind and have the same conversation with Alice again, I would change my question to one that was more open-ended and that sought to delve into her ideas, such as:

Alice:	My brain's a balloon.
Lisa:	How is that? Tell me more.

Or in this example, from an instance when Alice and her friend Isobel were blowing bubbles outside:

Lisa:	Why do you think the bubbles just burst like that?
Isobel:	Because they're not that strong and they can't fly really well.
Lisa:	Oh, why do you think they're not strong?
Isobel:	They're just sort of plastic.
Lisa:	What could make them stronger?
Alice:	Metal!

The purpose of my questioning here was not to get the girls to give me a response that I already knew. I was not trying to get them to guess what was in my head or what the adult explanation was. If that was my purpose, I would have decided that the bubbles burst because they connected with the grass, and I would have questioned until the girls gave me that answer. Instead, I wanted to find out what *they* thought about the bubbles bursting. I was interested in discovering their ideas, their emerging theories of the world. By finding out their schema like this, I got a view into their understanding or misunderstanding. I wanted to find out if they made connections between other phenomena and the bubbles (as Alice did in connecting her schema that metal is strong, so adding it would make the bubbles stronger).

Other times your purpose for questioning will be to scaffold young children's thinking so they learn to make a hypothesis. You will then want to guide them to think about the hypothesis in terms of their other knowledge of the world, or perhaps to support them to plan ways to test out their hypothesis. Your questions will then guide children to think through ideas, wonder about them, come up with a possible explanation, and then continue thinking or exploring the idea. In doing so, you guide children to learn *how to learn*.

The following conversation shows an example of how this might sound in your learning environment. A small group of children are making shadows by placing different items on an overhead projector, which projects the shadow onto a wall in their learning space.

Teacher:	How can we save this shadow?
Jason:	Can't save the shadow because the sun changes because it's dark at nighttime.
Caleb:	Turn off all the lights, we can't save it, then it goes away and put the lights on and it's a different shadow.
Brian:	Save if we draw it.
Chloe:	Yeah, draw it.

Teacher:	How can we work it out? Shall we try one of those things?
Brian:	We can draw it.
Chloe and Caleb:	Yeah!
Teacher:	So what do we need to get?
Caleb:	Paper. And markers. They'll work.
Teacher:	What kind of paper do you need? Let's go to the shelf and see which paper will be best.

The teacher supports the children as they choose the size of paper appropriate to the shadow they want to draw. He allows them to try two different sizes before they find one large enough to capture the whole shape.

On subsequent days this teacher could return to Caleb's original idea expressed here: "Turn off all the lights, we can't save it, then it goes away and put the lights on and it's a different shadow." He can ask the children, "How can we discover if the shadows are different each time we turn the light on and off?" His question provokes new thinking, stretches children's ideas about shadows, and also provides opportunity to learn strategies for exploring and researching.

Questions That Clarify and Focus Ideas

There will be times during conversations when you do not understand what a child is trying to communicate to you. Don't be afraid to say, "I don't quite understand. Can you tell me again?" or "I think I'm a bit confused. Tell me more about that." Within your secure and trusting environment and from your consistent interactions with them, children will learn this questioning for clarification is a normal part of conversation. They will become very comfortable clarifying or explaining their thinking to you because you are always interested in understanding *them*, not testing if they know something. They won't be like many of us were in our schooling, when we would freeze if a teacher told us he didn't understand. The children will understand that you see it as your responsibility to understand them. Asking children for more information is a powerful sign of respect for their ideas.

In order to clarify what a child is saying, it sometimes helps to rephrase what they have said in slightly different ways or using slightly different vocabulary. Often when we think aloud as adults, our ideas are not expressed in a succinct and clear way, and young children are no different. When you listen carefully beyond the words to the *ideas* the child is expressing, you can often support the child to bring clarity to her own thinking by rephrasing what she has said. This can clarify your own understanding and can also clarify the ideas for the child.

Be careful to choose vocabulary that children are familiar with, so that in rephrasing, the child's initial meaning is not lost or changed by words new to the child. This example is from a small-group facilitated conversation with some four-year-olds who were exploring shadows in a long-term inquiry.

Lisa (adult):	We looked at shadows in the playground yesterday, remember? So what about today? What do you see today?
Adam:	No shadows today.
Chloe:	Can't see shadows today.
Lisa:	Why do you think there are no shadows today?
Adam:	Cause it's raining.
Lisa:	Oh, it's raining?
Adam:	Yeah and all wet. My shoes got all wet.
Lisa:	[waits] Oh, so your shoes got wet when you came to school? [Adam nods his head]
Lisa:	[waits] So why do you think there are no shadows today?
Binh:	The sun takes them.
Areulia:	No sun.
Rachelle:	When the people walk, the shadows follow them.
Chloe:	The moon casts a shadow and that can make a shadow.
Rachelle:	I moved my hand and I saw my shadow come back!

As we can see in this example, it was a useful strategy to repeat the initial question. It helped other children participate in the conversation and to keep it on topic. Once you have allowed time for thinking, but silence and body language indicate there is no further information forthcoming, you can repeat the same question in a different tone or with different body language. You might repeat it more slowly, or with a more gentle or upbeat tone. You might repeat the question but turn your body to face other children if you felt that the question had initially been directed at one particular person. In repeating the question "Why do you think there are no shadows today?" my aim was to keep the conversation focused and to ensure the question had been given the time and thought it deserved. I wanted to find out what the children's ideas about shadows were, whatever they were. Their answers did not have to match my own ideas about shadows. I repeated the question to support the sharing of ideas. Repeating the question can give more thinking time and therefore more response and participation from the children.

You will also notice there were times where I waited before making my next response. It is a delicate balancing act to decide when and how often to repeat a question to focus the conversation or draw more children into it. The key is to know the children well. Then you will be better able to read their body language and understand their disposition and prior knowledge. These things will guide you to ask questions that support the conversation, rather than hindering it.

Questions That Connect Experiences or Ideas

We have explored an understanding of learning as making connections between prior knowledge and new experiences or ideas. Therefore, it makes sense to ask questions that will help children make such connections for themselves. Teachers can hypothesize about the connections children are making, but asking the children for their ideas or opinions provides far more information about how children are thinking. Listening to children's responses helps teachers see how clear these connections are within children's minds. Connecting questions serves as a bridge between experiences that can otherwise remain isolated activities. For example, the following conversation occurred when Isobel and Alice were drawing their memories of blowing bubbles in the backyard:

Isobel:	I'm drawing the bubbles.
Alice:	Me too.
	[silence for a few moments while the girls draw]
Lisa:	Do you remember what we saw inside the bubbles?
Alice:	A rainbow!
Isobel:	Yeah! A rainbow! I'm going to draw the rainbow now.
Alice:	I did a little bubble in another one. Remember when that happened, Lisa? It's the tiniest one. [referring to her drawing]
	[the girls continue to draw for a few minutes]
Lisa:	Where did the bubbles come from again?
Isobel:	We blewed them! I'm going to draw me blowing the bubbles now.

These questions helped the girls reconnect with a prior experience and sparked new ideas for their drawings. This next example shows questions that helped the girls connect their observations of the bubbles to their prior knowledge about the world:

Lisa:	Issy, what did you say about how the bubbles look again?
Isobel:	They're round.

Alice:	And they have rainbows.
Lisa:	Oh that's right, now I remember. [waits] So the bubbles were round. Hmmm . . . What does that make you think of? . . . The bubbles were round? Did they look like something else? [waits]
Alice:	A ball is round.
Isobel:	And one of them looked like the world one.
Lisa:	It looked like the world? How?
Isobel:	Cause it's kind of a jelly beans shape.
Alice:	Jelly beans? They're not round.

My questions were intended to stretch the girls' thinking about the characteristics of bubbles by asking them to think of how the bubbles are like other round things they know. Asking a question to connect their ideas to their knowledge about the world (in this case, about roundness) can support children's thinking across different experiences and begin to integrate their ideas (in this case, their ideas about the shape of balls, the globe, jelly beans, and bubbles). The question "Did they look like something else?" connects the bubbles to other round things without expecting a particular answer. The girls were open to respond with any kind of object, and their responses gave me new information about their schema. It led them to make a connection, but did not lead them to my own adult view of the world. At the end of this transcript, the girls proceeded to draw the bubble "like the world one" and Isobel showed us how the "jelly beans shape" referred to her image of land drawn on a globe.

Taking Ownership

Before your next facilitated conversation, ask a colleague to work with you to brainstorm a list of possible questions that could guide the children's conversation. Begin by writing all questions that come to mind. Reread and circle those that are open-ended and will help you delve deeper into the children's ideas. Which questions will help children make connections between their ideas or experiences? What kind of questions can you ask that will help clarify your understanding without leading children to your adult ideas?

Helping Children Develop Conversational Skills

Teachers play an important role in helping young children develop skills to success-fully participate in conversations. Jeanne Gibbs, in her book *Tribes: A New Way of Learning and Being Together,* talks of the importance of learning to listen, and says, "attentive listening is a gift to be given" (93). It is important for teachers to give this gift to their students, families, and colleagues. It is also important to teach young children skills in attentive listening so they, too, can give to others.

What skills are necessary to successfully participate in conversations? Adults often take for granted all the skills used in conversation, because participating in conversation is such a natural and integrated part of life for them. Being clear about the skills children need will help ensure you are providing ways for children to develop them. Conversational skills important for young children include:

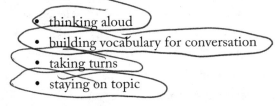

- thinking aloud
- building vocabulary for conversation
- taking turns
- staying on topic

Thinking Aloud

To be engaged in the type of conversations that reveal children's thinking, children need to be able to put their thinking into words. This requires more than just using words to name characteristics or recite facts. Some children are able to think aloud fairly easily, while others need more time, modeling, encouragement, and practice to do so. The most powerful way for you to help young children learn to think aloud is to think aloud yourself. Let the children into the secrets inside your mind. Show them what you are thinking about by talking about the questions, confusions, and ideas you have throughout the day. When you are looking at an interesting object or artifact together, ask your own questions: "I wonder what this is used for? I don't understand this, what do you think it does?" or "This reminds me of something I have at home. Look at the lines on the top. I think they look like the lines we made in the sand yesterday."

Your model immerses children in the language of thinking aloud. It will give them the words to think aloud for themselves. Always model your thinking aloud in a meaningful and authentic situation—that is, while you are involved in a learn-ing experience with children. Do not teach thinking aloud separately from all the other learning experiences in your program.

You might find that you need to model more for children at the beginning of the year, or for some children more than others. Think of gradually lessening your modeling as children develop skills in thinking aloud themselves and begin to use the language of thinking aloud. When you hear them say things such as "I wonder . . ." and "I think . . ." and ask questions about their experiences, you know you can concentrate more on listening to their thinking than providing a model of thinking aloud for them.

Building Vocabulary for Conversation

In order to fully participate in conversation, young children need a vocabulary of words known and understood. It is important not to assume that just because a child does not speak during a conversation, she is not participating through her listening and her thinking. But it still remains a goal of teachers to support young learners to develop their vocabulary for conversation. A rich vocabulary in early childhood has been identified as one of the most important indicators of later schooling success (Pellegrini 1985). It is important for building successful relationships in school and in life.

There are two avenues through which children develop vocabularies: contextualized language and decontextualized language. *Contextualized* learning experiences are those that make up many of the stories scattered on the pages of this book. Children learn new words while they are involved in conversations about real-life experiences. They learn new words as they hear adults and friends use the words in context. In conversation, these new words are often repeated more than once, providing a perfect context for learning vocabulary. The context of the conversation is essential for the new words to make sense to the child. The new words are also more likely to be remembered, recalled, and used later in an appropriate (and different) context because the child first learned them in a meaningful conversation that was connected to her learning and experience.

Decontextualized language experiences are those where the language is outside the child's immediate experience. They can include many of the vocabulary learning tasks traditionally found in schools, such as workbooks, flashcard drills, and finding dictionary meanings. These decontextualized learning experiences do not fit with a social-constructivist view of learning or with the view of a child as competent or capable. They do not help children transfer the learning of new words to other contexts, nor to connect their learning to prior experience. Moreover, they are not very exciting or engaging tasks.

Studies have shown that children most easily learn words

- that are important and meaningful to them (Markson and Bloom 1997).

  Our first words are often about our family and our most important needs, such as food and drink.

- that are conceptually connected to words they already know.

  Children connect new learning to their prior knowledge. Therefore, a child who knows the word "plane" might be more likely to learn and remember words such as "airplane," "aircraft," and "jet" (Bloom 2000).

- when they have opportunities to interact with objects associated with a new word, rather than just hearing the word (Wasik and Bond 2001).

  For example, a child will learn the word "train" when it is said while he is riding a train, or while he is actively playing with his toy trains.

Here are some strategies you can use to help children develop vocabulary to use in conversation:

- Be conscious of the words you use when talking with children.

  Embed new vocabulary in your language as children are involved in their active learning, ensuring your language is natural and meaningful to the activity. For example, while making fruit salad, use specific words when talking about the names of fruit and the tools and actions you are using. Rather than say "Pass me *those*," say "Pass me *the kiwi fruit*," or label what you see children doing by saying "I can see you're cutting the banana into slices. You're being very careful with the sharp knife." Balance listening to the children with your role in modeling new vocabulary.

- Use correct terms for objects and actions when you talk with children.

  For example, use the words "pupa" and "chrysalis" when studying the life cycle of butterflies.

- Use a wide vocabulary that is related to meaningful ideas in children's prior knowledge.

  For example, when playing in the dramatic play area, instead of "cooking," you can sometimes "bake," "grill," "fry," "prepare," "chop," or "toss."

- Plan to introduce new words as part of project work.

  When planning for a learning experience or inquiry project, brainstorm a list of possible words that can be naturally embedded into your language that will stretch children's vocabularies. For example, a study of trees might include words such as "trunk," "branch," "leaves," "roots," "soil," "earth," "buds," "sap," and "evergreen." Use these words in your language throughout the day so children hear them used in various meaningful contexts.

- Choose books based on their beautiful language and supportive illustrations.

  Many times, the illustrations of a book will support the understanding of new vocabulary. When talking about the book, use specific vocabulary from the text so children hear these words in another meaningful context. Use these words throughout the day in many different contexts.

- Use strong verbs, adverbs, and adjectives as well as nouns.

  Although children tend to learn and use nouns first, remember to embed and use verbs, adverbs, and adjectives in your language with children. For example, while watching a child painting, name what you see her doing: "You're painting such a long, thin line. It's very narrow. Look at those swirls you're making. They go around and around. I can see you're moving the brush very slowly."

- Use real-life props.

  When talking about ideas or reading aloud, use real items that children can hold, touch, taste, smell, and hear. Teacher Nancy introduced real-life building tools into the block area within an inquiry project about buildings. The three-year-olds in her class became very engaged playing and talking about the spirit level, tape measure, and rubber mallet. Sara, a librarian, visited different rooms to tell the fairytale of *The Three Little Pigs*. She used real-life props of sticks, bricks, and straw to support the children's understanding during her storytelling. Afterward, the children enjoyed playing with the materials in the block area, where they built their own houses and spontaneously retold the story using many of the new words they learned through Sara's storytelling.

Taking Turns

In the beginning stages of creating a culture of conversation, or for short periods of time, you might use specific strategies to help children take turns in conversation. I urge you not to rely on these strategies forever. You might use them only for whole-group conversations, and create more natural conversational structures during small-group conversations. A teacher's ultimate goal needs to be supporting children to learn skills and develop competencies in conversations without external structures. However, the following strategies will help you create a sense of what turn-taking is like and will help your youngest learners understand turn-taking with the assistance of a physical object.

- Use a speaking object.

  For example, try passing a large pom-pom, a small teddy bear, or a beanbag around the circle to signal whose turn it is to speak. I've seen stress balls (which are often given to teachers) used quite effectively here because they give children something squishy to hold and manipulate as they speak. Teach children that the person who holds the speaking object has his or her turn to speak and then passes it to the next person. Remember the power of your modeling, and hold the object when it is your turn to speak too.

- Go around the circle.

  Show how everyone gets a turn in order, giving children the opportunity to "pass."

- Use games to introduce turn-taking.

  Some teachers introduce turn-taking in this way through circle, board, or table games. For example, when a child plays a simple card game such as Go Fish or Memory with one or two friends, he learns to wait for his turn. Circle games such as Duck, Duck, Goose and Farmer in the Dell also help children learn how to take turns.

- Take turns boy-girl until everyone has had a turn.

  A review of research by Christine Howe (1997) highlighted the dominance of boys in all classroom interactions. The research showed that even when teachers believe they treat all children equally when choosing who has a turn in whole-class or small-group conversations, boys still make more contributions than girls.

This is partly because boys raise their hands more often than girls in whole-class conversations, and also because teachers often perceive boys' behavior as needing closer monitoring. You can create a pattern of taking turns boy-girl to help avoid this in your teaching. It also establishes a familiar and predictable environment in which everyone's participation is supported.

- Use conversational markers such as Popsicle sticks.

  Each child is given a small number of Popsicle sticks or small cubes (two or three work well). When the children have a turn speaking, they place their Popsicle stick in the center of the circle. When they have "spent" their sticks, they have "spent" their turns for that conversation. This strategy is helpful if you have one or two children who tend to dominate conversations, and encourages other children to participate. I've seen reluctant participants want to spend their sticks, causing them to participate in conversations more than they had before.

- Teach children to hold on to their idea.

  It's hard to wait your turn when you have something very exciting to share. Show children that when you ask them to hold on to their idea, you will return to them after the other person has finished speaking. If you do not do this, they learn that holding on to their idea isn't important. When you return to them as soon as the other person has finished speaking, they learn to remember their idea because they know they will get a chance to share it soon. I remember one teacher, Peggy, using a hand signal (which suggested holding something in her closed palm) to indicate to a child to hold his idea. This proved very effective for her as she didn't have to interrupt conversations to use it.

Staying on Topic

Staying on topic in a conversation can be a difficult skill to develop for children and adults alike. It is natural for our thoughts to wander off on tangents as we make personal connections during conversations. Make sure that your expectations are realistic. Are you expecting young children to talk about a topic for a reasonable amount of time? If the conversations of a group of three-year-olds go off topic after four or five minutes, this might in fact be quite appropriate. Ask yourself if you are expecting children to talk about something for too long.

Are your conversations about topics that are interesting and meaningful to the children? Reflect on what you are asking children to talk about. Choose topics that are of interest and meaningful to the children. The moments of conversation you offer throughout the day need to be about something relevant and meaningful for the children to want to participate, and in fact, to have something to share. Watch the children at play. What are some recurring themes? Do they show an interest in trains, doctors, or superheroes?

A visual aid often helps young children remember and stay on topic in a conversation. Help children connect and stay connected to the topic by showing photographs of the experience you want to talk about. Use a real-life artifact such as a pumpkin, leaf, or model train to connect children to the conversation topic as much as possible.

Summarizing the Conversation

Summarizing is a powerful strategy for many conversations, not just those with children. Periodically summarizing what has been said can keep the conversation on track and focused. It clarifies the children's ideas as well as the teacher's understanding. Summarizing reminds children of what has been said, acting like another memory for them. Sometimes the summary sparks more ideas or ways for other children to participate or connect their thinking. With careful language choice, the teacher can support connections without placing an adult perception over and above the child's developing schema. It is like a hint or a suggestion that the child can take up or not. One day, Alice and Isobel were discussing what it would be like to start school. I asked them how they thought school would be different from "kindy" (prekindergarten).

Isobel:	This is all the pages [points to her drawing of a book]. You learn to read at school.
Alice:	Now I'm going to draw me. Hello, Jasper [directed to her drawing of her dog].
Lisa (adult):	Is Jasper at school?
Alice:	No! You're not allowed to bring dogs to school, silly Lisa!
Isobel:	This is me and I'm reading the book. It's got lots of pages.
Alice:	I'm playing with the ball at school. And this is Daniel. And he's playing with a ball . . . I look kind of sad, don't I?

Lisa:	Oh, why are you sad?
Alice:	That's me and I look kind of sad because my head's a bit down, isn't it? I'm sad because no one will play with me with my ball.
Lisa:	What could you do about that problem?
Alice:	Ask if anyone would like to play with me?
Lisa:	Is that what happens?
Alice:	No . . . and this is my teacher.
Lisa:	So, this is you [pointing to Alice's drawing] and you're think-ing "no one wants to play with me," and this is Daniel, and this is your teacher.
	[Alice nods]
Alice:	She's looking after me.
	[the girls continue drawing quietly for a few minutes]
Lisa:	So, Isobel, you think that school will be different from kindy because you'll learn to read. Alice, you think school will be different because you'll play outside, and maybe no one will want to play with you, is that right?
Alice:	Yeah, but my teacher will look after me.
Isobel:	And my teacher will look after me too. And she'll tell me the words and I'll know the words.

When I said to Alice, "So, this is you and you're thinking 'no one wants to play with me,' and this is Daniel, and this is your teacher," I summarized what Alice had told us earlier in the conversation. It confirmed my understanding, but more im-portant, it also told Alice that I was listening intently to her. It told her I was inter-ested in her ideas. It also gave her the opportunity to revisit her thinking. She could hear her ideas again in a different voice. Summarizing the conversation like this is like revisiting a friend. Each time a child revisits her ideas, she gets to know them a little better.

A similar thing happened when I summarized both Alice's and Isobel's ideas with: "So, Isobel, you think that school will be different from kindy because you'll learn to read. Alice, you think school will be different because you'll play outside, and maybe no one will want to play with you, is that right?" But this summary also connected the girls' ideas with each other, and prompted Isobel to talk about her teacher too. Notice how I gave thinking time during the conversation. The girls were engrossed in their drawings, but I was really interested in their ideas about starting school, so I wanted them to talk too. Rather than asking another question to delve deeply, summarizing the conversation was another way to draw the girls back into conversation.

Using Memory Tools

Memory tools help connect children with ideas they explored or expressed at another time. It might be from earlier in a conversation or from a conversation or experience from another day. You can use their language or your statements and questions as a memory tool. Summarizing can act as a memory tool when the conversation is long in duration or rich in diverse ideas. You might make a statement that connects children to a previous experience or conversation. For example, you might find yourself saying:

> Jonas, I remember that at the start you were worried the girls would knock over the helicopter pad you built. How do you feel now?

> Do you remember when we went to the beach and found all that seaweed?

> Remember when Precious brought the bird nest to school?

Teacher language is one tool that helps children remember and be connected to previous learning. Other concrete memory tools also work effectively to reconnect children and provide them a chance to revisit their ideas. The following memory tools invite children into new conversations about their ideas, and allow them to think more deeply about them:

- reading scribed conversations to children
- listening or watching recorded conversations with children
- looking at photographs from experiences with children
- looking at memory objects from experiences with children

Reading Scribed Conversations to Children

Many teachers use a previous conversation to spark a new conversation with children. Teachers Marilla and Ellen effectively used this technique when they scribed a conversation about windows while on a walking trip. During their morning meeting the next day, Ellen read the transcript to the group. The children picked up on the idea of looking through the class window to draw what they could see. Reading the documented conversation allowed the children to explore their ideas about windows more deeply, sparked an idea for a motivating learning experience, and drew new children into the exploration of windows. Reading scribed conversations at the start of whole-group or small-group conversations offers an effective introduction to the topic of a facilitated conversation.

Listening or Watching Recorded Conversations with Children

Playing a section of a recorded or videotaped conversation instantly reconnects children to the initial experience. They hear the words and remember them. They can revisit them at greater depth as they are now a little removed from them. In a similar way to how Ellen and Marilla read the conversation transcript in their morning meeting, a recorded conversation or videotaped learning experience can be used as a memory tool for children.

Looking at Photographs from Experiences with Children

When celebrating a special event such as a birthday, a family celebration, or a vacation, we often capture the experience in photographs to help us remember the event. Taking photographs of learning experiences conveys the same message to children: this is an experience worth remembering. Every time we look at photographs of that special family dinner, for example, we are reminded of the people there and the events that took place. We also remember how it felt to be part of the celebration. Looking at photographs of learning experiences with children will remind them of the events, the feelings, and the ideas they experienced.

During a field trip to observe a nearby construction site, teacher Nancy took photographs to capture the experience. She used the photos during whole-class and small-group conversations, helping the children reconnect with their initial experience. By looking at the photographs, the children were given the opportunity to revisit their thinking, as one revisits with a dear friend. Each opportunity to view the photos brought out more thinking and language. The children noticed new things and bounced off each other's ideas. The photographs linked them back to the experience, becoming a tool for remembering and also a catalyst for further and deeper learning. Facilitating a conversation about the field trip without the photographs would have proven more challenging to Nancy and the children.

Looking at Memory Objects from Experiences with Children

Young children often feel more connected to an event or experience (and to their thinking about it) when they can see or interact with an object from that experience. For example, to help young children feel secure and connected to their family, teachers often suggest children bring a favorite soft toy from home to school. A transitional object helps children connect the two places. Similarly, objects from initial learning experiences, like cookie baking or a neighborhood walk, can instantly reconnect children to those experiences. Perhaps this is the appeal of the souvenirs many adults collect on their travels. These objects help us recall memories of vacations and travels whenever we look at them.

Some ideas for using memory objects to reconnect children with earlier experiences are:

- Use recipes, utensils, or containers from a cooking experience to spark a facilitated conversation, or place them in the dramatic play area.
- Place a familiar book on the drawing table or painting easel. Use a known story as a catalyst for a facilitated conversation about a particular topic.
- Ask visiting experts who visit your learning environment if there are any objects they could lend (or that may be inexpensive to buy) that will help reconnect children with the experience. Do the same when you are on a field trip. Examples of objects include a shell from the beach, fish food from a pet store, tongue depressors from a doctor's office, leaves from the park, the foot-measuring instrument from a shoe store, or chopsticks from a Japanese restaurant.
- Keep the shopping lists you use when shopping with a small group of children for the ingredients to make fruit salad.

Bringing Conversations to a Close

It can sometimes be difficult to judge when to end a conversation. Time constraints or interruptions sometimes dictate when a conversation will end, but ideally you will work toward children's conversations being limited by external forces less and less. Sometimes children will clearly tell you when it is time to conclude the conversation, usually through their behavior. When you see children begin to lose focus on the topic—perhaps by showing more interest in what is happening at the painting easels or by focusing on the shirt of the person sitting next to them—take it as a cue that the conversation is no longer working well. This is your message that it is a good time to end the conversation. Avoid too much external managing of children's behavior. When you read the signs given to you, you get information about the interest level of the children in regard to a particular topic. Aim not to scold or reprimand a child if she loses interest or gets wriggly in a class meeting or conversation. She is more than likely telling you something with this behavior, not purposefully trying to sabotage "your" meeting time. Yes, teachers need to have high expectations of children and support them as they learn ways to listen and speak to each other, but not in a way that forces participation in something that holds little meaning for them. How many times have you been to a meeting as an adult and had a difficult time staying awake, keeping still, or staying focused? We acknowledge that this is natural behavior for an adult when the topic, pace of conversation, ideas, tone, climate, or other factors (emotional, physical) may stop us from fully participating. So why is it any different for a child? Why do we expect that these things are not important to participation just because the participants are four years old?

If a child or small group shows they can sustain a conversation for only short periods of time, start small and slowly build the duration of your conversations together. Challenge yourself to hypothesize about what might be stopping them from more fully participating. Is the topic really of interest and relevance to them? Are you choosing the environment carefully so distractions are limited? Are these children feeling unsure of using English? Are there other symbolic languages that may be more successful in helping them express their ideas? Will it be easier for these children to talk about their ideas while they are involved in a learning experience rather than at a small- or large-group meeting? Will the child who does not participate in whole-class conversations be more comfortable participating in small-group or partner conversations? Will it help if you use a concrete artifact or prop as a memory tool for connecting experiences or as a stimulus for conversation?

Taking Ownership

Think of a recent learning experience in your learning environment. If you wanted to reconnect children to this experience so you could facilitate a conversation about it, what would be an effective memory tool?

Conclusion

A culture of conversation is rich in conversational moments. The voice of the children is the focus. When you enter these learning environments it is often difficult to find the teacher as he is usually in amongst the children, interacting with and listening to them. This does not mean your role is any less than the teacher who is up front directing children's activities. In fact, for the teacher who is interested in children's ideas, his role is far more complex and often more challenging. There are always new strategies to learn and new skills to develop. Your commitment to listening intently to children also requires a commitment to thinking deeply about your own teaching and to continuing your own learning about the craft of teaching.

The strategies explored in this chapter will help you begin and then continue this journey of improvement and enrichment. The first step is to pause. Teachers have such busy days, and supporting the learning of young children is a nonstop physical, emotional, and intellectual job. Teachers need to learn to pause and step out of this "busy-ness" so they can reflect and make goals for improvement. Pause and reflect on ways you facilitate conversations now. Reflect on ways you listen closely to children. Become more conscious of the questions you ask. Be aware of the time you give children to think before you continue the conversation. Become more aware of how you might unintentionally lead children to your ideas instead of to exploring their own schema. Pause first. And then become a more consciously skilled teacher by reflecting on your role as a listener to young learners.

References

Bloom, P. 2000. *How Children Learn the Meanings of Words.* Cambridge, Mass.: MIT Press.

Gibbs, J. 1995. *Tribes: A New Way of Learning and Being Together.* Sausalito, Calif.: CenterSource Systems.

Howe, C. 1997. *Gender and Classroom Interaction: A Research Review.* Glasgow, Scotland: Scottish Council for Research in Education.

Markson, L., and P. Bloom. 1997. "Evidence against a Dedicated System for Word Learning in Children." *Nature* 385 (6619): 813–15.

Pellegrini, A. D. 1985. "The Relations between Symbolic Play and Literate Behavior: A Review and Critique of the Emperical Literature." *Review of Educational Research* 55 (1): 107–21.

Wasik, B. A. and M. A. Bond. 2001. "Beyond the Pages of a Book: Interactive Book Reading and Language Development in Preschool Classrooms." *Journal of Educational Psychology* 93: 243–50.

CHAPTER FIVE

Collecting Conversations

During a conversation, children's words float in the air like the soapy bubbles Alice and Isobel blew in my garden one day, temporary and fragile to the touch. When written down, words become more concrete and permanent, able to be touched and visited again and again. The process of documenting conversations, particularly transcribing a conversation, can make the ideas of children more visible through their words.

When I first read in *The Hundred Languages of Children* about the way teachers in Reggio Emilia document children's language, I must admit I wasn't completely sold on the idea. It seemed like an awful amount of work to me. It still seems like a lot of work (because it is), but I now see how enlightening the process can be for revealing the ideas behind the words.

Usually I am too busy facilitating a conversation, writing down the children's words, or listening carefully to really interpret more than what first jumps into my mind during a conversation. This means I often make the same kinds of interpretations or the same kinds of connections over and over again, as I fall back on my established habits of making meaning as a teacher. With the children's words in front of me, written on paper, I can return to them time and time again. Each rereading offers a new opportunity to see things not revealed before or to interpret in new ways not imagined before. As the Reggio Emilia educators say, documentation makes "visible the ways of learning" (Rinaldi 2001, 83). Writing down children's words makes their thinking more tangible and accessible for deeper interpretation.

This chapter covers strategies and systems for collecting children's conversations. The ideas will help you make decisions about:

- what to collect
- when and where to collect
- how to collect
- how to zoom in to focus your collecting

What to Collect

Documenting children's conversations while teaching can be challenging. It is impossible, and unnecessary, to capture every conversation that occurs in your educational setting. You would end up spending most of your time documenting, and not very much time interacting with the children.

Instead of trying to capture everything, carefully choose which conversations you will document. Consider the balance between spontaneous and facilitated conversations. Are you interested in following a particular group's thinking about a topic? Are you trying to capture some conversations for each child in the group over the year? Think clearly about your goals for collecting conversations.

Be prepared for the unexpected and be ready to document those magical times when children surprise you, but also be purposeful about your documentation so that it will be meaningful and beneficial to your understanding of the young learners in your care. Here are some ideas for documenting conversations:

- Choose one child to follow for a week.

  Decide to document one child's conversation once a day wherever he is when you have the time to listen closely. It might be at the sand table one day, while on the computer with a friend the next day, and during lunchtime another day.

- Follow one small group of learners.

  Choose a group that is exploring ideas around a topic or concept. It might be the group of four girls building the snowflake factory, the trio who love to spend time watching the new fish swim in the class aquarium, or the pair who play hospital almost every day. You will still interact with other children, but you will collect the conversations of this group to interpret further with your colleagues. Think about what is manageable for you. It might be realistic to document one conversation every two days or one each week. You have control, so make it work for you and your context.

- Commit to documenting two or three conversations each week.

  Some teachers keep themselves on track by marking on a calendar when they have documented a conversation. Once you find something interesting in one of these conversations, you might like to follow the conversations in that learning area or with that child for a while.

- Choose one type of conversation to follow for a few weeks.

  Perhaps you are interested in collecting small-group conversations for a few weeks, or following the one-to-one conversations you have with children. Maybe you want to focus on collecting spontaneous conversations between the children, or facilitated conversations that help you see your role more clearly. You can collect examples of one type of conversation to look at more closely or to work out if you spend conversation time with each child over time.

When and Where to Collect

Making decisions about when and where you will collect conversations will help you manage your workload. You can choose a certain area of your learning environment (where) or a certain time of the day (when) to collect conversations. For example, you might decide to listen to and document conversations at one of these places or times:

- at the painting table
- at the science discovery table
- as children construct in the block area
- during your morning meeting when you bring a mystery object for children to guess its use and purpose
- during mealtimes
- after reading aloud to children

How to Collect

It is helpful to establish routines, systems, and strategies to make documentation efficient and manageable. The more simple and straightforward the system of record keeping, the more likely you will be able to keep it going and use it successfully. Many teachers are able to organize their teaching life with elaborate record-keeping files and record-checking systems, but personally, the more bits of paper I have to coordinate, the harder it is for me to stay organized. This section explains the following techniques for collecting conversations:

- scribing
- recording
- transcribing

Scribing

Scribing children's words as they talk is probably the easiest documentation technique to establish, but perhaps the most difficult one to maintain. Learning a new habit requires commitment and determination, but if you believe it serves an important purpose, it is far more likely to succeed. Make it easy by deciding on a method that will work for you. You might need to experiment with a few strategies before discovering your best fit. Some teachers place notepads or sticky notes with pencils or pens in different areas of the room so writing materials are always close at hand when they hear an interesting conversation. Other teachers place clipboards with paper and pen attached in these areas so that they are accessible and easy to use. Some prefer to have one notebook where they jot all their observation notes and transcribe conversations. Others wear a pen around their neck and carry a notebook in an apron pocket.

Scribing conversations can work particularly well when listening to spontaneous conversations. During this "eavesdropping," because you don't need to concentrate on facilitating the conversation or think of a question to ask next, you will have more time and focus to put into scribing children's words. It also allows you to view children's relationships and interactions independent of adult involvement and intervention.

Here are some tips for scribing children's words:

- Write the children's words exactly as they say them. Do not be tempted to improve the grammar or structure of their words. Honor and respect the words as you do the speaker.

- *Always* write the date. It can also be interesting to record the time of the conversation, for future reference and interpretation.
- Record the names of all of the children who are present. Make sure you write down the name of every child who is part of the conversation, experience, or play, even if a child does not speak. Nonspeaking children are still part of the experience.
- Write a brief context statement. Even if this is only a phrase, it will help you and any other readers place the conversation in a meaningful environment.
- You might not need to scribe the whole conversation. An interesting phrase, a question from a child, or a brief interaction between two children might give you just as much insight into their thinking, ideas, and use of language as a longer conversation would.
- In a team-teaching situation, allocate roles. For example, one teacher can facilitate the conversation and another can scribe. This works well for a whole-class meeting. When possible, have an adult volunteer scribe as you facilitate a conversation. This can be a way to increase meaningful family involvement.

Taking Ownership

Next time you decide to be in the moment with a child or small group, take a notepad and pencil with you. As you listen, write down what the children are saying. Don't worry if it doesn't seem significant at first. The words might reveal their potential to you later, or they might not. Consider this your time to practice scribing children's words as you listen. Don't forget to write down the date and a brief idea of the context (such as "At the block area" or "Drawing flowers").

Recording

Recording conversations with a voice recorder or video camera allows you greater freedom to focus on the children's ideas and be in the moment with them than scribing does. Without the pressure of trying to keep up with writing everything down, you can relax into the process and perhaps engage more completely with the children's ideas than if your energies are spent writing. This makes recording an ideal documentation tool for facilitated conversations. Ned, a teacher of three-year-olds, sees it this way: "I slowly realized that I was focusing more on *my writing* than on the children's words. Sometimes when I read my documentation, there really wasn't that much that I felt I could use. I think I was writing just because I thought I had to write, rather than being purposeful about it. So I'm going to put the paper away for awhile and tape some conversations to listen to later. I think it will help me focus more on the children and on the kind of questions I'm asking."

Recorded conversations can be transcribed at a later date or replayed both for adults and children. It is important to remember how valuable it is for children to revisit their learning experience. Replaying conversations for children not only delights them when they hear their own voices, it also provides an opportunity to remember an experience and to reconnect with it and their thinking that day.

Don't be surprised if the first few times you play a recorded conversation to children all they do is giggle and notice who is talking. Many adults do this too the first time they see themselves on a video or hear their voices on tape. Don't get anxious about this or annoyed with the children for not listening with care to "your" tape. With frequent exposure, they will become accustomed to it and will then be in a place to listen more carefully to the words and ideas of the conversations. The worst thing you can do is stop playing the tapes to them. If you stop, the children will never get to the stage of feeling familiar with this experience.

The videotaped or recorded conversation has great value as a record of the whole conversational experience and gives you the chance to interpret nonverbal language, tone, and expression in ways scribed conversations cannot. There are many small voice recorders on the market that offer unobtrusive ways to record spontaneous and facilitated conversations. Many small and relatively inexpensive digital cameras also provide the capacity to take video of ten or so minutes, providing the memory card is large enough. You can place a video camera on a tripod in the corner of the room so you are still free to facilitate the conversation or work in other areas of the room.

For example, Stacy, a teacher of three-year-olds, set up a video on a tripod to record the children in her room working with clay over a number of days. From viewing the videos later, she noticed a pattern of creating and talking about flying things: airplanes, butterflies, and rocket ships. The information from the videos gave Stacy the starting place with a small group of children for an inquiry into flying machines.

Taking Ownership

Choose a facilitated conversation that you hope will open up children's thinking to you. Voice record or videotape the conversation. Later in the day, revisit the conversation by listening to or viewing it again. What are your initial feelings and reflections? What is the tone of the conversation? Do you think it achieved the purpose you set for it?

Transcribing

Once the technology is in place, it takes little time and effort from the teacher to record conversations. It does, however, require much more time and energy to transcribe these experiences so they can be further interpreted. Remember that it is neither realistic nor necessary to transcribe every conversation you record.

For example, while researching the way children explore clay as a new medium for thinking, Dave, Peggy, and I would view and review videos of the children at work during our meetings. We did not transcribe the children's language, but were still able to gain new insights into their learning with each new viewing and pedagogical conversation. Each time we viewed a video piece again, it revealed new ideas, questions, and wonder for us. While a transcript might have revealed other parts of children's thinking that we didn't notice in the video, it was still a meaningful pedagogical conversation for us without the transcript.

You may also decide to transcribe only part of a conversation. A fifteen-minute group conversation or play experience may yield only three or four minutes of conversation that are valuable to transcribe. For example, Rose and Jason set up a video camera to document children's block play and Rose's interactions with the children while they were working. During their planning meeting, they viewed the twenty-minute video and decided to focus on two sections of the tape that were later edited to a few minutes each. Reviewing these edited sections allowed them to focus their transcribing on a child's independent problem-solving process. They then looked at the most effective questions teachers can ask to support problem solving without giving the child an adult solution.

Here are some tips to support you as you transcribe conversations:

- Engage the help of families and other volunteers to type the transcripts.

  Caregivers who work out of the home and cannot be part of the daily school experience are often interested in helping in other ways that will fit into their schedules. Preschool teacher Gail ensures she says each child's name as she facilitates a conversation that is being recorded so her parent typist will know who each voice belongs to. Taking a photograph of the experience will also help the volunteer identify the children participating.

- Make typed transcripts easy to read.

  Use a double space between lines and a tabbed indentation at the start of each new paragraph. Typing into a table and then hiding gridlines and borders is an efficient way to achieve this. Experiment with fonts and sizes to find which work best for you.

- Transcribe as soon after the event as possible.

  This helps your memory aid in the process. If it's not possible to transcribe immediately after the conversation, include a photograph to show the context and identify the children, helping you connect with the initial experience.

- Add information such as body language and tone to bring life to the words.

  Before or after typing children's words, include their body language or tone in parentheses, such as (leans forward) or (in angry tone).

- Consider including a photograph or a sketch of the experience.

  For example, a sketch of the block construction the children are talking about or a photograph of the pasta machine they are discussing on the field trip to the restaurant will complete gaps of missing information for the reader and interpreter (see the photograph on the following page).

How to Zoom In to Focus Your Collecting

The above suggestions will help you get started documenting conversations. Earlier, you began listening more intently to the young children in your learning environment by spending a few minutes alongside them in the moment, practicing how it is to be a teacher who listens before she talks. Now you can begin the process of capturing conversations by beginning in a similar way: by taking small steps and building on your successful experiences.

Once you have tried one or two of the previous suggestions, you will find yourself ready to dig a little deeper into the fascinating world of young children's thinking. Imagine this phase of your journey like using a magnifying glass: you have a taste of the wide view, have become comfortable with one or two systems, and now you want to zoom in on a particular area so you can study it more closely.

Date: 3/12/06	Children:
	Daniel & Eamon
Observer: Lisa	Thomas – joined later & built independently
Context: Choice Time Block area	

	Teacher Reflection
1. Daniel & Eamon building on their own, then joined together.	
2. D: "making a tower with eyes" made 2 similar towers side by side	Why did it have eyes? Was it 1 or 2 towers to Daniel?
3. E suggested connecting these 2 bldgs c̄ his bldg. He made a "road" from his structure to the towers	Eamon's strategy for connecting play – to build structure which connects bldgs ∴ people playing also connected
4. Together built another "baby tower" in front of the "tower w. eyes"	
5. added red string on baby tower. Made "mouth" & "elevator".	Will they continue building together? Why human features on buildings?

Including a sketch helps to fully capture the learning.

You can magnify a particular area or interest by thinking about what you want to document before you sit down with the children. It helps to make a list of your own questions about the children's learning. What are you curious about in this area or with this group of learners? What are you wondering? For example, before documenting the conversations at your drawing table, your list of questions might include:

- How does the children's talk influence what they draw? Do they borrow ideas for their drawings from the conversation topic?
- Do the children talk with each other about what they are drawing, or do they talk about unrelated topics?
- Do the children talk about the method of drawing—that is, do they talk about *how* to draw, not just what they are drawing?
- Does the environment I've created nurture and encourage children to talk with each other?

Getting in touch with your own questions and curiosities will help you dig deeper into children's conversations and learning. Your list of questions needs to be dynamic and fluid—your questions about collecting conversations from the drawing table in a few weeks or months could be quite different from the ones above.

This process helps you focus your thinking and focus the lens of your collecting. It guides you to make decisions about what you will document and what you will leave, and also helps you decide the best system for this documentation.

Let's take the drawing-table example a little further. You have already decided *where* to collect conversations (the drawing table). Let's say you next decide that listening to the children's spontaneous conversations will help you explore some of your questions. You have decided *what* to document (spontaneous conversation), so at first you will not facilitate or participate in the children's conversations. This helps you decide *how* to collect the conversations. You decide that scribing the conversation will be an appropriate system to use. It is easy to manage, and because you're not facilitating the conversations, you will be able to quickly grab your notebook or clipboard when you see children together at the drawing table.

You decide to keep your notebook near the drawing table so you are ready when the children are. The first few times you scribe, the drawing-table conversations will give you more information about the effectiveness of this system, and if you find it hard to manage, you can change the plan and use a small voice recorder. Perhaps you find your attention being diverted by other children and you can't fully concentrate on the conversations at the drawing area. In that case, recording the conversation and listening to it later will relieve some stress for you.

The first few scribing sessions will also give you general information. You will probably scribe everything you hear and see at first. This will tell you about the children's topics of conversation and may help answer some of your questions. It will probably create new questions for you too. However, you might also discover you want to zoom in even more and document only the conversations in which children talk about the methods of their drawings, for example. You have used the magnifying glass to determine what to study more closely. This allows you to be very clear about what you will and won't document. You will listen carefully to the whole conversation, of course, but for the purposes of delving into the children's thinking, you will document only the discussions you are most interested in.

Taking Ownership

Choose an area of your learning environment or a child or group of children you are curious about. Make a list of your questions and wonderings. It helps to use the question starter "I wonder . . ." when making your list. Use your list to guide your decision making:

- *Will you document spontaneous or facilitated conversations?*
- *What tools or system will best fit with this environment and your purpose? Can you scribe, or will you need to record conversations so you can be free to facilitate the conversation?*
- *What specifics will you listen carefully for and document? Do you need to document your interactions as well as the children's? Do you need to document the conversation throughout the process or only the children's conversations explaining what they did?*
- *Make a plan and begin. Remember to be flexible and modify this plan as you get new information from your learners through their documented language.*

Conclusion

It is important to reiterate that not *all* conversations will be worth documenting, and not all documented conversations will illuminate amazing theories from children's thinking. Some conversations are just pure fun and silliness. Sure, these, too, might offer insights into children's thinking, but not always. When beginning to value and document children's language in these ways, teachers sometimes feel deflated because they are not hearing the kind of conversations they had dreamed of. Sometimes this is because the teachers' skills in interpreting conversations are still developing, or the topic of conversation is not connecting to children's interest or prior learning. Perhaps the children are still learning how to be in a learning environment that values their talking and their ideas, and so the culture of conversation needs time to grow.

At other times, however, teachers just expect too much. They are already hoping for certain kinds of responses and ideas before they have even listened to the children. They have such high expectations because they know their children are smart and curious and capable. But if you expect every conversation to be filled with gems, your expectations might be unrealistic.

Remember that the conversations you read about in books (including this one) have been selected for the purpose of telling a story or highlighting some learning. There are many other conversations that were not included in books because they did not show the thinking quite as well. In a similar way, not every minute or second of a conversation will be worthy of deeper interpretation and reflection. In a ten-minute conversation, there might be less than two minutes of interaction worth transcribing. Sometimes only one line or phrase from a child is significant, lifted from a longer conversation or overheard as she was engrossed in painting, reading a book, or climbing on the playground. Keep alert for these moments by showing your genuine interest in the children, and you will be ready to document them for further study.

References

Edwards, C., L. Gandini, and G. Forman, eds. 1998. *The Hundred Languages of Children*. Greenwich, Conn.: Ablex Publishing.

Rinaldi, C. 2001. "Documentation and Assessment: What Is the Relationship?" In *Making Learning Visible: Children as Individual and Group Learners,* Project Zero & Reggio Children. Reggio Emilia, Italy: Reggio Children.

CHAPTER SIX

Interpreting Conversations

After spending time creating conversational moments throughout the day, learning strategies to facilitate the kinds of conversations that reveal children's thinking, and capturing a conversation by scribing or recording it, you will want to make use of it. A documented conversation is filled with possibilities waiting to be revealed. What can it tell you about the children's emerging theories about the world? Are the children connecting ideas in interesting or unexpected ways? Do their words show some confusion (or misinterpretation) about concepts or ideas?

This chapter will help you interpret the conversations you collect:

- making meaning from conversations
- working in collaboration with your colleagues and the children's families
- strategies for interpreting children's words
- interpreting the teacher's role

Making Meaning from Conversations

There are many ways to make meaning from a conversation. It is important to be open to different ways of understanding children's words, and to view each conversation as a whole rather than just as a series of isolated parts. Only then will you have given the children's ideas the respect and care they deserve.

When teachers interpret a conversation, they seek to bring out the meaning of the speakers. They search for understanding but not necessarily a definitive explanation. They build hypotheses. When interpreting conversations, your thinking about children's and teachers' words must always remain open to further possibilities and not be fixed on one explanation of its meaning. *Your* way of understanding the conversation is only *one* way to make meaning of it. This understanding can also change with time and reflection. Your ideas about a conversation might change from one day to the next.

Conversations are relational: the speakers interact and their ideas interact. Therefore, it is important not to break up a conversation too much, but to view it as a whole, where the individual words, phrases, and interactions can bring different meanings to different listeners (and readers). Because effective learning is often a social activity, it is not possible to view each speaker in isolation. Rather it's necessary to seek understanding about the ways in which their interactions support one another's growth and learning.

Working in Collaboration with Your Colleagues and the Children's Families

While you will gain interesting insights from interpreting children's conversations on your own, you will gain more by interpreting them with others. By talking through it with others, you reap the benefits of having others' perspectives enrich or challenge your ideas. The way other people interpret and understand the children's words might be different from yours, stretching your ideas and pulling you out of routine ways of understanding children. If they are similar, this can be useful to your learning also, affirming your knowledge and understanding and helping you make connections between your prior knowledge and experience. You can learn a lot about the children, their learning, and your teaching from interpreting conversations with your colleagues and with the children's families.

To help illustrate this point, let's look at an example of a collaborative interpretation involving three teachers who work with the same group of three- and four-year-olds:

Date: March 28, 2005	**Documented by:** Marilla

Context: Morning Meeting. Children have arrived to school wet from walking in the rain. Ellen is facilitating the meeting which Marilla documents. Ellen asks children about the rain and this is one part of the conversation.

Interpreted by: Ellen, Marilla, Lisa   Planning Mtg

Ellen: What is rain?

Jonathon: Rain is little drops that's water. It's cool 'cause it gets on your head.

Andy: Rain is big drops that fall on your head or on your umbrella.

Maria: If it's raining you need a umbrella.

Johanna: Rain doesn't fall on your head because you wear a hood on top of your head.

Monece: If it's raining you have to use a umbrella. Rain drops on your head.

Ben: Rain is drops.

Does J mean "cool" as in "cold" or as in "fun"?

Are rain drops always big? Can/Are they different sizes?

Umbrellas, hoods... have children all used umbrellas themselves or is their experience second-hand from adults?

"Drops fall": from where?

tomorrow: use this conversation as a memory

Possible next steps:

Conversations to explore chldn's theories of where rain is from. Could lead to exploring diff. clouds & water cycle. How can we measure rain drops? Explore chldn's ideas first. Possibilities: paper to catch first drops? How??

Umbrellas — how do they work? Draw, observe, use diff. umbrellas. Handles, designs, springs, open & closed views Design own umbrella ... What doesn't use umbrellas? Why? Can we make an umbrella for them?

⟶ good concrete materials. Start c̄ this.

An example of notes made during interpretation of documented conversation.

Teacher Helen asks the following question to a small group of children, following up on a conversation from the previous day: Where does the rain come from?

Agnes: From the clouds and the sky.

Jimmy: Rain is kind of like water that comes from the sky and it's like those funny drops.

Mack: The rain splash and the sun become moon.

Molly: Rain comes from the sky and the snow.

Sophie: The snow melts and the snow becomes rain. And the clouds start to drop rain.

Jacki: The clouds.

Maryann: They come from clouds inside it. And birds can cover them in trees. When they have a wind the birds can't fly.

During the subsequent meeting to collaboratively interpret the conversation, the teachers had different perspectives about the meaning held within the children's words. The following pedagogical conversation took place. Notice the difference of opinion among the teachers. See how this becomes a source of intellectual conflict to stretch their initial interpretation or hypothesis about the children's words.

Helen: Why do you think Jimmy thinks the drops are funny?

Ian: Funny? I don't get that either. Where would he have seen drops that could be funny?

Helen: Maybe he means funny more like unusual or interesting?

Ian: I'm trying to picture raindrops in my head . . . I can't imagine them being funny or unusual.

Michelle: I think that's because we have an adult view of raindrops already conditioned. Jimmy sees the raindrops as funny because his ideas are more open than ours. We've forgotten how to see things differently, but our kids show us how to all the time.

Helen: I never thought of it like that. You're right! I keep trying to make sense of it through my eyes and my definition of funny. But this is Jimmy's definition. I still don't understand what could be funny about raindrops though.

Ian: So we have to find out from Jimmy. How could we do that? Shall we have another conversation with him?

Michelle: Or we could ask him to draw what he meant by those words . . . read him the transcript and ask him, "What did you mean when you said 'those funny drops?'" I'd love to see how he would draw them.

Ian: But what about Mack's comment about "the sun become moon"? What does he mean? It sounds like he has some strange confusion about the sun and the moon to me.

Helen: Oh, I don't see it that way. I thought it was his way of saying the moon replaces the sun at nighttime.

Ian: Oh, maybe. But he has confusions about other things too. Remember when he said the wind came from the leaves the other week?

Helen: Yeah. I've been thinking about that though. I don't think it's necessarily any confusion about the ideas or concepts. I think it might be that he's learning English and this is the best way he can describe his ideas in English at the moment. I don't think we should jump to conclusions that he doesn't understand until we explore it more with him. Otherwise we might be assuming the wrong thing, just because English is his second language.

Ian: I'm not sure I agree . . . but I get what you mean about his English. Hmm . . . what about if we do the same thing with him and see if drawing will help him explain it more clearly to us?

Michelle: It's worth a try. But maybe we need to include him in more conversations too and just keep digging a little deeper to find out what he means. I think he needs us to spend more time with him one on one.

STEPS FOR INTERPRETING TRANSCRIBED CONVERSATIONS

1. The teacher who documented the conversation gives some context for the other adults, such as the names of the children involved, the time of day, where the conversation took place, and the purpose, topic, or initiating experience for the conversation.
2. All adults silently read the transcribed conversation as a whole.
3. Each adult takes the role of a child, and together they read the conversation aloud.
4. Take time to think about the meaning behind the children's words (see hints on page 136).
5. Share your initial thoughts with your colleagues. What do you notice?
6. Read, read, and reread! It is important to spend time with a transcript if you believe there are interesting or thoughtful ideas expressed in the conversation. They might not reveal themselves to you immediately.

Working with Colleagues

Colleagues who work together already understand much of the context of a particular learning experience or conversation. Even when not all the teachers were involved in a conversation, when they work with the same group of children they already know the children, their relationships, and probably their family background and educational experiences. Each person will bring his or her unique insight and prior knowledge to the interpretation, but it will be bound together by a common understanding of the context of your early learning setting. This makes your colleagues ideal collaborators to interpret the conversations that you document.

Throughout this book, we are exploring the importance of creating conversational moments for children's learning. Teachers also benefit from conversations with each other. The most effective and enriching way to interpret children's conversations and plan for their learning is through pedagogical conversations with your colleagues. In the collaborative setting of pedagogical conversations, teachers can help each other listen carefully to children's words, see the schema they reveal, and plan ways to stretch children's thinking.

Pedagogical conversations do not happen by accident. It's essential to create time, space, and opportunities for teachers to talk with one another. Time—or the lack of it—is often the critical factor in early learning settings. Teaching is a profession where the work is never done—there are always competing demands on your time. However, a commitment to learning through conversation with children is fully effective for teachers and for children only when time is set aside to talk with colleagues.

Evaluate your own context to determine the best ways to create a time, place, and opportunity for pedagogical conversation. Making time for pedagogical conversations will speak volumes about how teachers are valued and how their right to their own learning is respected at your center. Early learning settings have found various ways to create this time, including:

- naptime for preschoolers.

  Teachers can sit with one another in the classroom while children are sleeping.

- weekly staff meetings.

  Instead of an administrative agenda, it is possible to create staff meetings with a professional development focus.

- evening meetings.

    Teachers can meet after children have gone home, perhaps committing to one night a week.

- teacher preparation time.

    Also called non-contact or non-instructional time, one prep time each week could be dedicated to sharing children's conversations.

Prioritizing time for teacher collaboration is rarely an easy task, but teachers who believe they can learn from talking with and listening to their colleagues (and that the learning of the children will be enhanced because of it) will commit to finding creative and ingenious ways to meet. Teachers who take on this commitment often find that their work is easier and more enjoyable because of the collaboration.

If you work alone with a small group of children in your home, or if your colleagues aren't as committed to this area of learning as you are at present, it may not be possible for you to create a collegial group for pedagogical conversations. See if there are like-minded teachers in your neighborhood or network group to gather for discussions. Some teachers find that Internet support groups and listservs are helpful if they don't have colleagues to work with one-to-one.

Interpreting Conversations with Families

While we often have more opportunities to engage in collaborative interpretations with our colleagues, interpreting documentation of children's conversations together is a uniquely rich and meaningful way to work with a child's family. Families will often have prior knowledge about their child's experiences that you do not. This knowledge can help you better understand a child's thinking. By understanding families' potential contributions, teachers can change their view of how the teacher-family (or home-school) relationship can be. They can imagine new possibilities, which can be empowering both for teachers and families.

There are a multitude of reasons why it can be difficult to establish effective relationships with families: the negative experiences of a family member's own schooling, language differences, working family members who are not able to be as involved in their child's school life, differences in philosophies and beliefs about learning, distances traveled by children to school, and so on. Begin by acknowledging the one thing you have in common: the child. Even when families' ideas about teaching and learning differ from the teacher's, they, too, are coming from a place of concern. They, like all teachers, want the best for their child. Beginning with this common ground can be a starting place for developing true partnership, and transcribed conversations can be a bridge between these two worlds. Just as the transcripts make the child's learning visible to us, they will make the learning visible to the family too.

During parent-teacher conferences, Jane, mother of four-year-old Izzy, met with Izzy's teacher, Nancy. They shared many stories and reflections about Izzy, including a drawing of a house and the accompanying story Izzy had created that week. Izzy had said the house had a "strange wall." Nancy wasn't sure why it was strange to Izzy but Izzy didn't explain it further. As soon as Jane read her daughter's scribed language, she said, "Oh, I know what that is. She's talking about our summer house. It has a large glass sliding door, but it looks like a wall of glass and Izzy was really intrigued by it last summer." Immediately, Izzy's artwork and words became clear to Nancy. Jane's prior knowledge of Izzy's life experience put a missing piece of the puzzle in place for her. This story shows the power of teachers and families working together to interpret children's language. Family members have unique perspectives and prior knowledge to bring to the interpretation, and the teacher who is open to listening to these as closely as she listens to the child will gain much more insight into the child's life. In turn, the family will gain greater insight into the child's life at school, as a learner, as a thinker, and in relationship with others. Rather than parent-teacher conferences, which are often one-way conversations directed by the teacher in the role of sole "expert," transcribed conversations can help school-family relationships to more fully become a collaboration to support the child.

Taking Ownership

Next time you transcribe part of a conversation, make a point of sharing it with the child's family. Ideally, this would happen at your early learning setting, where you and the family members can sit together and read the child's words. Be conscious of your body language. Be sure to sit alongside the family members and not apart or above them. You are seeking to form a reciprocal relationship, not one where you are the only expert. You might say something invitational like, "I thought this was really interesting. What do you think Ben means here?" instead of launching into your own teacher-interpretation of the child's words. This kind of conversation may take just a few minutes, but will work wonders for building positive relationships between home and school.

Strategies for Interpreting Children's Words

So how can we make meaning of conversations? What do we actually do to interpret children's words? The following strategies can help you understand young children's conversations:

- visualizing
- questioning
- making connections to prior knowledge or experience
- synthesizing chunks of information

Visualizing

Whether we are listening to them or reading them, words interact with our prior knowledge and we build personal mental images of meaning. When we listen to a conversation or read a transcript and focus on the mental image created, we can better understand the meaning of the words. Visualizing helps us make sense of children's words. This strategy is particularly helpful when it is difficult to understand what a child is saying. You might understand the words on a superficial level—because you know what each word means, and they are not nonsense words—but need to work a little harder to understand what these words mean together or how they connect to the topic. By concentrating on making a mental image of what the child is saying (seeing, hearing, feeling, smelling, and perhaps even tasting in your imagination), you can gain a better understanding of what a child is trying to communicate. For an example, let's look at the words of three-year-old Izzy:

> For Mommy and Daddy. With the house, on the roof. The door. It got four lines on it and a strange wall. And trees.

While reading this I find I need to visualize each part Izzy is talking about. If I don't make an effort to create a picture in my mind—of the house, then the roof, the door, and so on—I don't get a clear idea of what Izzy is saying. Visualizing helps me more fully understand the ideas within Izzy's words.

Taking Ownership

Try the strategy of visualizing for yourself with four-year-old Daniel's explanation of making a lava lamp:

Actually with the oil it actually worked, but it doesn't go on forever. The oil just goes up with the water. The water pushes it up and it is amazing. When you shake it, the water goes around and the bubbles go around and then they go up again, it is a bit like an oil spill, because the oil actually flushes out of the ship and into the sea and makes the whales and penguins die. Water and oil don't mix, so when you do this you won't believe your eyes!

Next time you find yourself struggling to understand what a child is trying to tell you, focus on the mental image the words create in your mind. What do you visualize? See if this helps you make meaning from the words.

Questioning

Asking questions of yourself when looking at a transcript of children's conversations is different from asking children questions in order to clarify or delve deeper into their thinking. This form of questioning happens within your mind as you listen to a conversation or read a transcript. As you listen to or read the words, you ask yourself questions. These questions help you search for understanding. Your questions might alert to you that you aren't sure what a child is saying ("Hang on, what does she mean?") or they might alert you to possible connections being made ("I wonder if she thinks the tree needs more water because she helped the principal water her plants yesterday?" or "Perhaps she thinks the fish can't see because she doesn't open her eyes when she goes underwater?"). Your questions might also alert you to an area of your own curiosity ("How interesting . . . I wonder what she knows about electricity?" or "I wonder if she has a picture in her mind about how her brain works?").

The following example shows Natalie's transcribed explanation about a toy horse she collected for her treasure box. In parentheses are the collective questions from a small group of teachers, documented as they interpreted the transcript. Many of the questions were asked during the interpretation, when the teachers read and reflected on the transcript. When they reread the transcript, they wanted to understand it more deeply, and so used the strategy of questioning to help them do so. By focusing their thinking on asking questions about Natalie's ideas and words, the teachers were able to think more divergently and see more of her meaning in the transcript. Their questions helped them listen more deeply to Natalie.

I have a horsey. *(Does she mean a real horse or the toy one?)*

I got it from my daddy. Daddy's last name spells with a "C." He got the horse downstairs. *(Does her dad's name have a "c"? Does she mean his last name or last letter? Or first letter? What is her schema about names, letters, and words? Does she mean downstairs at the school or at home? I'm still unsure if it's a real or toy horse.)*

His name is Suji. *(The horse's name?)*

He is one years old. *(Does that mean she got him one year ago or does she know the horse's actual age? Or is it a reflection of her understanding of age?)*

It's a carousel horse.

Do you know how they go up and down? *(Perhaps we can ask Natalie to draw the carousel for me. I wonder how she might show the up-and-down movement in her drawing.)*

And once I went to Central Park with my mommy. Everyone was on that carousel and I wanted a turn. And I choosed this horse. *(Did her mother buy her the horse while they were at Central Park?)*

And there was music and it went "doo doo doo" and it was going very fast and I had to hold tight. *(Was she scared? I wonder if she can show us how she looked when she was holding tight. Would drawing or clay be a good material to explore this? Would looking at her face and making different expressions in a mirror change her representations of how she looked? Did she remember this experience because of her feelings when holding on tight? Why was this such a memorable day for Natalie? Was it an unusual event to go to Central Park with her mother?)*

And Mommy told me that too.

Making Connections to Prior Knowledge or Experience

Another strategy to make sense of spoken or written text is to make connections between the words and your experiences or prior knowledge. As you read a transcribed conversation, you can search for connections between these words and prior experiences of the child. Possible connections might be:

- Do these words or the ideas expressed connect to the child's experience from another day? Do they connect to an experience at school or at home?
- Do the ideas connect to something you know about this child as a learner, thinker, or communicator?

- Do they connect to knowledge you have about the child's family or other relationships?
- Is it possible that the child is connecting these ideas to one of these prior experiences? Perhaps you are not aware of a certain experience or prior knowledge of the child, but does this conversation with him make you want to find out a little more about his experiences outside of school?
- Is it possible that this child is connecting his thinking to words he heard in a previous conversation, either from adults or another child?
- Do any of the ideas connect to each other, either within the words of one child or within the interactions of the children conversing?

Remember, you are not trying to name, label, or identify what the child is *definitely* connecting in his thinking, but it can be helpful to consider possible connections he is making based on your own prior knowledge of him. Keep open to possibilities: think and talk about them as possibilities and interpretations rather than as an absolute rationale for the child's thinking.

It is helpful to talk with teachers and other adults who know the child in different contexts. Their different knowledge of the child might bring different connections and interpretations. Is there a teacher who only sees the child on the playground? Or a visiting storyteller who interacts with the child once a week? Perhaps seeking out the child's teacher from a previous year will help reveal connections to a child's prior knowledge and experience that you are unaware of. Just as when Nancy met with Izzy's mother (see page 130), acknowledging and valuing the different prior knowledge others have of the child brings greater depth to your interpretations of the child's words.

One day, five-year-old Jason told his class during morning meeting that he knew all about "composing." His teacher documented the conversation but had trouble making sense of what Jason meant by "turning" and "it's not smelly." She wasn't aware of a musical background in his family, and then a week or so later a chance conversation over lunch with the school gardener revealed that Jason liked to visit him almost every day. It turns out, Jason and the gardener often talked about the compost that was made for the school gardens. It wasn't *composing* that Jason knew about, it was *composting*! Be open to being surprised by children, and also by the people who have a different view and prior knowledge of them that can help with your interpretations.

Synthesizing Chunks of Information

Sometimes it is not until the end of a conversation, or at least not until after a certain amount of time listening, that you will have that "a-ha" moment of understanding. When listening carefully to a child, working very hard to understand the ideas she is trying to communicate, we sometimes need to suspend the desire to know what she means immediately. Only after a few chunks of information are we able to piece these parts together to form a meaningful whole. Quite often, the chunks of information can come from different speakers as they interact with each other and their ideas are shared, built upon, and transformed. Synthesizing these chunks into a meaningful whole idea is an important strategy to develop and use when making sense of children's conversations. This is how you interpret a conversation as a whole, see the child as a whole person, and understand how each child's thinking happens within a social learning environment. Without synthesizing the chunks of the conversation, you run the risk of seeing only a narrow view of what the child's schema or ideas are.

When rereading a transcript, it's helpful to ask yourself how the different parts of the conversation are connected to each other. You can integrate the meaning, making strategies of visualizing, questioning, and connecting to prior knowledge to create a synthesis of understanding. Let's look at Natalie's horse conversation again. It has a good example of an "a-ha" moment when ideas are synthesized. I have included my internal thinking during the process of interpreting her conversation below. It shows how my understanding evolved or emerged throughout my reading, and my efforts to understand how the chunks of information relate to each other in order to create a meaningful whole. If I had stopped my interpretation too early or not synthesized the chunks of information, I might have formed a less accurate idea of what her horse conversation was about.

> I have a horsey. *(Does she mean a real horse or a toy one?)*
>
> I got it from my daddy. Daddy's last name spells with a "C." He got the horse downstairs. *(Now it's about her dad? No, it's still about the horse.)*
>
> His name is Suji.
>
> He is one years old.
>
> It's a carousel horse. *(A-ha! So it must be a toy horse then! I have the mental image of a small stuffed toy.)*

Do you know how they go up and down? (*Oh, so she really does know something about carousels. She's seen a carousel somewhere that goes up and down, I guess.*)

And once I went to Central Park with my mommy. (*Oh! Okay, the carousel is at Central Park.*)

Everyone was on that carousel and I wanted a turn. And I choosed this horse. And there was music and it went "doo doo doo" and it was going very fast and I had to hold tight.

And Mommy told me that too.

Synthesis of the conversation as a whole: Natalie remembers the experience of riding the carousel horse very well. She remembers how tightly she had to hold on, so it was an important event to her. The toy horse represents her experience riding the real carousel in the park with her mother.

HINTS FOR INTERPRETING TRANSCRIBED CONVERSATIONS

- Visualize the children in conversation. Doing this will help you follow who is speaking.
- Visualize the ideas expressed by the children. This will help you understand what they are thinking.
- Notice your inner thinking (metacognition). What parts make you curious or puzzled? What parts do you find yourself attracted to or returning to? Why could this be?
- Wonder about the ideas expressed by the children. Hypothesize what they might be thinking about, curious about, or confused about.
- Make connections. Are any ideas in this conversation connected? Do they connect to prior experiences of the children? Do they connect to your knowledge of these children?
- Synthesize the conversation as a whole. What meaning have you made after the complete reading? What are the main ideas expressed by the children?
- Listen to your colleagues' ideas and perspectives. How are they different from your thinking? Can they offer you an alternate way of understanding learning?

Thinking About the Words

The above strategies are useful for interpreting possibilities for learning and for listening to ideas within or beyond children's words, but they are not the only ways to interpret a conversation. You might find that one or two of the strategies help you the most and you use them consistently. Or you might choose to focus on one or two to delve deeper in understanding particular conversations. For example, you might decide to collaboratively interpret a transcript with a colleague by asking as many questions as you can generate. This alone might give you enough insight and possibilities for further exploration. For a different conversation, one that is proving a challenge to understand, you might use visualization and focus your thinking on creating mental images to help you uncover the child's meaning.

Other conversations will reveal certain words that stand out from the others. Sometimes children have ways of expressing themselves that do not necessarily need deep interpretation, but might just need to be noticed for their beauty or particular perspective on the world. For example,

- Do the words show a use of metaphor, analogy, or poetic language?
  › "My brain is like a balloon." (Alice, four years old)
  › "The lights are dancing." (Nicholas, six years old)
  › "The shadows play with each other all day." (Jonah, four years old)
- Do the words show an unusual way of viewing the topic?
  › "Why can't the fish see the hook in the water?" (Nicholas, six years old)
  › "How does the elevator know to stop?" (Ethan, four years old)
- Do the words show humor?
  › "You can't have dogs at school, silly Lisa!" (Alice, four years old)
  › "You haven't drawn any pants. The teacher with just underpants!" (Charlie, seven years old)
- Do the words or tone show a sense of awe or wonder that may offer new possibilities to explore?

Mary:	Oh my gosh! The butterflies!
Melina, Ella, Mattie:	Yeah! Yeah! Yeah!
Ella:	Let's clap!
All:	[clapping and yelling] Yes, yes, hurray, hurray!
Ella:	We have to tell Ellen! What is her telephone number? I don't know!
Kristie:	I don't know why there are butterflies?
Ella:	Oh, look at the beautiful butterflies! Hip, hip, hurray!
Mary:	It's so beautiful!
Mattie:	I'm happy! He flying?

Taking Ownership

Take a transcript of a conversation from the children in your learning environ-
ment. It doesn't matter how long or short it is. In fact, it is probably useful to
start with a short transcript. Sit with your colleagues and use the strategies
explored in this chapter to interpret the conversation. Visualize, make con-
nections, ask questions, and come to a synthesis of understanding about the
conversation as a whole. What did you discover about the children?

Interpreting the Teacher's Role

It is important to occasionally spend time reflecting on the role you are taking in
facilitated conversations. A powerful way to do this is to document a conversation
that includes your interactions with children by voice recording or videotaping the
experience. The documented conversation will give you the chance to ask questions
such as:

- What kinds of questions did I ask?
- What other strategies, such as summarizing and repeating, did I use?
- Did the questions help uncover more thinking?
- Were any questions leading the children to think in a certain way?

Doing this can be a little frightening because it can challenge teachers' percep-
tions of themselves as educators. Sometimes teachers want to believe they always
do the "right" thing. They think they should know how to do everything and be an
expert at it all just because they are teachers. In reality this is clearly not possible,
nor is it healthy to think of teaching as never needing to improve. Teachers today
are challenged to change this view of themselves. They are challenged to become
educators who are constantly learning and honing their craft.

You can meet this challenge with confidence by taking the following steps:

- Interpret your role on your own first.

  One way to feel more comfortable interpreting your role in conversations is to begin by interpreting on your own. Most teachers are
  more critical of themselves when interpreting their role in conversations, so beginning on your own will help you feel more confident
  to reveal this part of your teaching to your colleagues.

- Focus on the questions, not the questioner.

    Interpret and critique the questions, not the person asking them (you), so that the critique is taken from the personal to the objective. Questions can't have their feelings hurt or ego damaged.

- Look at the interactions, not just your (the teacher's) words.

    Rather than focus solely on your words, ensure that you interpret the children's words before and after them. Conversations are dynamic and relational—individual comments do not sit like an island alone. It is particularly important to look at what precedes your interaction with a child, not only what response a child gives to your question.

- Slowly bring your colleagues into the interpretation.

    Share the responsibility through a roster system in which each teacher takes a turn bringing a conversation to collaboratively interpret.

Let's look at an example from Rose, teacher of three- and four-year-olds. She wanted to look more closely at the role she played in supporting children's learning in the block area, so she asked me to join her in interpreting video documentation she had collected. By focusing on the questions, not on Rose as a person or a teacher, the interpretation became less personal and more helpful to Rose. The interpretation asked the question "What *interactions* (including questions) were most helpful in supporting problem solving, in drawing out children's ideas, in encouraging the tentative player?" It did not ask "What did *Rose* do that was helpful (or not helpful)?"

Rose was invited to share her reflections first: What questions did *she* notice that supported the children to follow their plans and not take over? Teachers are often their harshest critics, and so beginning with Rose's own reflections eased the awkwardness of interpreting her teaching practice. Next time, it was another teacher's turn to bring a transcript that included her role to interpret together.

Taking Ownership

Watch or listen to a recorded conversation at home one evening or weekend when the house is empty. Get used to seeing and hearing yourself from another perspective. Then move on to viewing or listening to the recorded conversation with your colleagues. Show them you are open to improving because you want to do your absolute best in facilitating conversations with young learners.

One final way to create a safe and secure environment for you and your colleagues is to use a predictable process. We talked about the importance of structure for young children in chapter 3—and teachers also benefit from predictability, particularly when embarking on a new area of pedagogy. Try the process suggested in the following list when interpreting a teacher's role in conversations with your colleagues. It will provide predictable steps for you to follow and create a safe environment for you to interpret the effectiveness of your role when facilitating conversations.

PROCESS FOR INTERPRETING THE ROLE OF A TEACHER:

1. Read the whole transcript to yourself, in a collaborative setting if possible.
2. Adults take child and teacher parts and read the transcript aloud to ensure understanding of the conversation as a whole. Use comprehension strategies such as visualizing, connecting, and questioning when understanding breaks down.
3. Highlight teacher interactions. Number them for easy reference.
4. Use the form template found in appendix A as a guide to collaboratively decide the purpose for each teacher interaction by reading the transcript before and after each highlighted interaction. Ask the teacher in the transcript to talk about what he or she was thinking or wanting to achieve when that interaction took place. You may need to add new sections to the template.
5. Write the number and teacher language on the template, according to the purpose of the interaction. For some interactions there may be multiple purposes or different perspectives from the interpreting group. You may need to document some interactions more than once.
6. Look for patterns. Were more interactions for certain purposes recorded? Which interactions seem to fulfill their purpose? Were some interactions ineffective in their purpose? Did some interactions cut young learners off or lead them to an adult idea that may not have been their own? Are there different or more effective ways to ask certain questions?
7. Summarize the interpretation. What did you learn from the process of interpreting teacher interactions? How will this influence the way you facilitate conversations?

Interpreting the Teacher's Role: An Example

One day I met with a small group of kindergartners for a facilitated conversation. I was interested in their ideas about thinking and was curious to find out as much as I could about their schema. I voice-recorded the conversation so I could concentrate on facilitating the conversation rather than writing down the children's words. This documentation also enabled me to interpret the language and questions that were most effective in drawing out children's thinking. The following is the transcript of this conversation and the subsequent interpretation on my role with teachers Dawn and Vanessa:

> Jordi, Leo, and Polly (five-year-old kindergartners) with Lisa (teacher)
> Monday, March 26, 2007

Lisa:	What happens when you think? (1)
Leo:	You get a lot of guesses.
Lisa:	Oh. . . . Tell me more. (2)
Leo:	And when you think, you know some stuff.
Lisa:	You do? (3) [waits] What kind of things? (4)
Leo:	And when you think you could tell the teacher some right stuff.
Jordi:	We learn something new—nonfiction books and we are paying attention to the teacher and we learn something good.
Lisa:	So what happens when you think? (5)
Jordi:	I like the part. I don't like the part.
Lisa:	Oh, they are the things you are thinking? (6)
Polly:	This reminds me of . . . This part is funny.
Jordi:	I wonder why?
Polly:	You forgot one . . . Zara's picture. [shows me how Zara looks when she is thinking "oh" and pointing to something in a book]
Lisa:	Oh, so they are the things you are thinking about when you are reading a book? [waits and children confirm this understanding] (7)
Lisa:	So . . . which part of your body does that thinking? (8)
Polly:	Your brain.
Lisa:	Your brain? Where's your brain? (9)

Polly:	Inside your head.
Lisa:	[waits] What do you think it looks like in there? (10)
Leo:	Right now I'm thinking!
Lisa:	Right now you're thinking about what it looks like inside your head? Wow! (11)
Leo:	[nods and smiles]
Jordi:	I thinking too. When you have brains you . . . [unsure] . . . If you don't have bones you couldn't do things, but if you have bones you can do things.
Lisa:	[waits] So, what do you think, Polly? You said that the brain is inside your head. What do you think it looks like? (12)
Polly:	Pink . . . dark pink.
Leo:	I think it's like a line and it's like a circle like this. [shows me]
Lisa:	So what do you think happens to your brain when you're thinking? What do you think your brain does? (13)
Jordi:	The brain know how to teach us.
Lisa:	Oh . . . so how does it do that? [Leo raises his hand]
	What does it do, Leo? (14)
Leo:	Our brain, it learns something new and it tells us something we don't know.
Polly:	When we thinking then it comes to us and then we know.
Lisa:	How interesting! Do you think if you got a piece of paper and a marker, you could draw what you think the brain is doing? (15)
	[children go to get materials]
Polly:	It helps you where to go.
Jordi:	The brain talk to us and the brain will help us.
Lisa:	How does the brain talk to you? (16)
Jordi:	But he's inside? But is really really has to call louder so it know it can hear us.
Lisa:	Oh, so the brain has to call loudly so we can hear the brain? Is that what you mean? (17)
Jordi:	[nods]
Leo:	No, no. It just comes up our head and we say it.
Jordi:	[drawing] And I draw the face.
Leo:	Brains don't have no face.
Jordi:	Well that's my [vacation?] and I on [vacation?] . . . I only the one, because I wasn't here.

Leo:	That's the circles like this . . . that's how the brain looks.
Jordi:	He's thinking and he's helping. The brain's inside my head and I'm going to draw my head.
Leo:	Now I'm going to label it. [his drawing of the brain]
Jordi:	That's me and that's the brain inside my head.
Lisa:	What are you thinking about in that picture? (18)
Jordi:	I'm thinking and the brain hear me and the brain said I will help you if you say the magic words. And you have to say the magic first.
Polly:	The brain is talking to me.
Lisa:	What is the brain saying? (19)
Polly:	Tell your mum and dad and your sister and brother . . . to say I love you.
Leo:	[reading his labels] Brains help you think.

CATEGORIES OF TEACHER INTERACTIONS

Date: 3/26/07	Participants: Jordi, Leo, Polly (Teacher: Lisa)
Context:	
Facilitated conversation:	

Supports child to join in play, learning experience, or conversation	So, what do you think, Polly? (12) What does it do, Leo? (14)
Supports child to problem solve	
Clarifies teacher understanding of child's idea or thinking	Oh, so they are the things you are thinking about when you are reading a book? (7) Oh, so the brain has to call loudly so we can hear the brain? Is that what you mean? (17)
Affirms or encourages child's efforts/ thinking/work	You do? (3) Right now you're thinking about what it looks like inside your head? Wow! (11)

CATEGORIES OF TEACHER INTERACTIONS (CONTINUED)

Wonders aloud (models questioning)	
Models curiosity	Tone of voice Body language: leaning forward to children; eye contact with child speaking How interesting! (15)
Stretches child's thinking (challenges or provokes)	Which part of your body does that thinking? (8) What do you think it looks like in there? (10) Do you think if you got a piece of paper and a marker, you could draw what you think the brain is doing? (15)
Seeks information about the immediate *(for example, asks to retell, to describe or to label parts of child's work if drawing or blocks)*	Tell me more. (2) What are you thinking about in that picture? (18)
Delves deeper into children's ideas	What kind of things? (4) Your brain? Where's your brain? (9) So what do you think happens to your brain when you're thinking? What do you think your brain does? (13) So how does it do that? (14) How does the brain talk to you? (16) What is the brain saying? (19)
Connects to prior experience, or is a memory for the child	You said that the brain is inside your head. (12)

Gives the child an adult solution to a problem	
Leads child toward the teacher's idea	So the brain has to call loudly so we can hear the brain? (17) *In seeking to clarify, could this be leading Jordi to my idea of the brain more than his?*
Brings conversation back to the topic	So what happens when you think? (5) What do you think it looks like? (12)
Other	

Summary of Teacher Interactions

During our interpretation, Dawn, Vanessa, and I decided that overall most of the teacher interactions fulfilled their purpose and supported the children in sharing their ideas about thinking. I was aware I used my prior knowledge of this class's literacy program when I made the connection between Jordi's words and strategies for thinking and talking about books (7). This prior knowledge helped me make sense of what Jordi was communicating to me. At first I wasn't sure what he meant or where he was going with his ideas, or in fact if they were at all connected to the question I had posed about thinking. I needed to listen closely and not jump in too soon, and in doing so was rewarded by this connection. This illuminated both Jordi's connection for the word "thinking" to his schema about thinking, and my understanding of his words.

Dawn and Vanessa noticed that I gave thinking time and gave Jordi the opportunity to elaborate on his ideas. We did wonder, however, if I had unintentionally led Jordi to something that was more my idea than his when I sought to clarify my interpretation of his words (17). It is important that I be cautious and aware of this and monitor whether my interactions tend to follow this pattern. Dawn, Vanessa, and I also discussed how important it is to continually infer meaning from the children's words so that our conversations with children are natural and free-flowing. We decided that raising our awareness of leading questions and being conscious of our own adult ideas about the topic were important to the way we facilitated conversations. But we didn't want to stop asking questions that clarified our understandings. Teachers need to feel safe to take the risk and ask these clarifying questions so conversations can keep flowing naturally.

After interpreting this conversation with Dawn and Vanessa, I decided that I wanted to document further conversations. I plan to particularly watch for times when I might lead children to my ideas, rather than uncovering their own. The idea of asking children to draw their ideas was a spontaneous one, but considering how successful it was in highlighting the children's thinking to me, I would definitely choose to use it again.

Taking Ownership

Record a facilitated conversation that includes your interactions. Use the template in appendix A to interpret the purpose for each question or interaction. What patterns emerge? What kind of interaction happened most often during this conversation? What questions seemed to help bring out children's ideas? What questions were not so helpful? What will you do differently next time you facilitate a conversation? What will you be more conscious of continuing to do in conversations?

Before beginning your next facilitated conversation, brainstorm a list of possible open-ended questions and other statements based on what you learned from interpreting your interactions. Use this list as a guide rather than a script for the conversation.

Conclusion

This chapter is about spending time with the ideas children have expressed in conversations. Interpreting and thinking deeply about young children's words will reveal their schema and their thinking to you. The most effective way to do this is within a collaborative relationship with the child's family and with your colleagues. This is why it is so important to create a culture of conversation not only for the young learners, but for you, your colleagues, and the children's families. These pedagogical conversations will be the context for you to develop your skills in guiding, documenting, and interpreting quality conversations, and will help you bring new practices into your teaching.

CHAPTER SEVEN

Listening to the Child with Developing Language

In most early childhood learning environments there are children who do not express themselves easily or readily with words. It might be because they are shy or cautious in new situations, or it might be because their expressive language is developing. Their first language might be different than the primary language of your learning environment. It is our challenge as teachers to find ways to listen to their thinking. In fact, teachers need to make a larger commitment to understanding these children because their thinking might not be immediately accessible. Teachers might not hear these children's ideas through their expressive language as they do the ideas of other children. Their words might not reveal to teachers their schema about the world.

So how can teachers listen to these children, if not with their ears? That's the topic of this chapter. It will explore ways to understand children with developing language, ways to include these children in conversation, and strategies for uncovering their thinking through imaginative play, block construction, and drawing.

Understanding the Quiet Child

The quiet child is often overlooked in a group of excitable and gregarious learners. He challenges his teachers to work harder to understand him and get to know him. Teachers need to be cautious about assumptions they might make about the quiet child. To do this, you need to:

- Build a complete picture of a child before assuming he is unable to participate in conversations.
- See the child as having the potential to learn language and to participate in conversation.
- Understand that the child might understand language even if he does not speak it.
- Value the participation of listeners as well as speakers.

Some children have a shy disposition or feel uncertain when things change, which leads them to be listeners more than speakers in conversations. This can sometimes be a cultural value; in some cultures, children are expected to listen to adults and not question or talk to them first. Only by developing close relationships with each child and with each child's family will you be in a position to know this. Create times to talk with each child's family, and listen carefully to them. Is the child different at home? Does the child contribute to family discussions? What is the family language? How does the child react when in unfamiliar situations? What is the child's history? Did the child easily learn to speak, or were there some difficulties noticed by the family? Build a complete picture of a child before jumping to conclusions that he or she cannot or will not speak.

Teachers who view all children as having the potential for learning language and participating in conversation continually strive to find ways to draw in the quiet child. They value how the quiet child can participate by listening, and they understand that even if a child chooses not to speak, he is often thinking about the topic being discussed. They search for other ways to listen to the quiet child's ideas, and consistently encourage and nurture his participation in conversation. These teachers would not exclude the quiet child from opportunities for small-group conversations. They continue to ask him questions in whole-group meetings, sometimes asking him questions directly in a gentle and encouraging tone. They show interest in him. They continue to gently invite participation, knowing that the quiet child has the potential to learn language and be involved.

Teachers must be cautious not to assume that a child does not understand language just because they do not hear him speak it. It is widely accepted that when learning any language, receptive language abilities develop faster than expressive language. I definitely found this to be true in my own meager attempts to learn American Sign Language (ASL). After a number of months of immersion in ASL during my work with PS 347, I was able to understand some general conversations or a teacher's lesson, but I still struggled with my expressive abilities. Even now I understand a lot more than I can sign. The child with developing language is the same. His English might include many confusions and errors. His vocabulary might be limited and his understanding of the grammatical structures of English developing. His English might be difficult for you to understand, but it is essential to remember that he undoubtedly understands a lot more than you hear him speak.

Finally, value the role of the listener in conversations as you do the role of the speaker. While your ultimate goal needs to be to draw the quiet child into conversation and to foster the development of language for the English-language learner, understand that he is still participating even when he is not speaking. Teachers sometimes assume a child is not participating when in fact much thinking is happening as he listens to the ideas of others. This chapter will show you some other ways to listen to the ideas of this child, and in doing so you will connect with him and be in a stronger place to draw him into conversation with you.

Taking Ownership

Think of a quiet child in your group. What do you know about the child? What do you know about the child's family? Write a list of ten things you know about this quiet child. Now write a list of things you want to discover about the child. How can you set about finding out?

Including Children with Developing Language

You can implement specific strategies to include children with developing language in conversation. The first step is to gain a full picture by listening to the child's family, and then ensure that you:

- accept the child for who he is
- focus on his strengths and abilities, not on what he *isn't* doing
- continue to invite and encourage participation
- are patient
- think about the times and places you invite his participation
- find ways to provide conversations in a child's first language

I remember Laura, a six-year-old I taught many years ago. Laura refused to speak to anyone at school: me, other staff members, her friends, other children, or other children's parents. Her family assured me she was quite the chatterbox at home. She seemed to enjoy school and participating in the learning experiences presented to her, except when she was asked to talk about them. Laura's mother assured me she talked about school at home and never put up any fight to come to school in the morning. She played with other children in the classroom and also during recess and lunchtimes. We were all puzzled about why Laura chose not to speak at school.

Rather than make a fuss about it, I decided my strategy would be to accept Laura for who she was. While I remained concerned she was not participating fully in the life of the class, I continued to encourage her to be a contributing and valued member in ways she felt comfortable. I didn't make excuses for her. I continually invited her to speak about her experiences, but when she refused (usually by giving no response at all), I would wait patiently for a moment and then move on. I thought if I made a fuss about her not talking, it would draw attention to her "not-ness": it would make Laura into "the child who doesn't talk" rather than being "Laura who loves drawing, butterflies, and making patterns." I didn't want her to be defined as a deficit. We got on with the life of the class. The children accepted Laura for who she was, and she continued to be part of their games and play.

I still remember the feeling of surprise and awe I experienced on the day Laura spoke for the first time in class. We were holding a class meeting, and from the corner of my eye I noticed Laura's hand raised in the air. I was so excited, I had to work very hard not to cut off the child who was speaking and go immediately to Laura. She gave her brief comment, and the class meeting continued. It seemed the other children knew, too, that this was a milestone for Laura, and I could tell they were pleased for her by the smiles on their faces and the rapt attention they gave her, but they didn't overwhelm her with expectation either. I was astounded she would choose such a public arena of a whole-class meeting to speak. I had assumed if and when she did speak, it would be to one friend, or perhaps quietly to me when no one was near. Laura didn't miraculously begin speaking all the time at school from that day on. She continued to be quiet and reserved, but interacted more freely with her peers and very occasionally would share her thinking in words. The lesson for me was in patience and in believing that *every* child is capable of being a fully contributing member of the learning group.

In understanding the child in your care who may not speak during conversations, you might want to think about the times you ask him to contribute. Are you focusing only on whole-class conversations? Are other children taking the airtime from the quieter children? Would it be worthwhile to facilitate some small-group conversations to see if it helps the child feel more comfortable speaking? Who would be best to include in this small group? Establishing small conversation groups with children who will support rather than take over for a quiet child is an important consideration. You may feel it better to include some children who will be models of language. Or you may believe it will be more secure for the quiet child to be with the two or three children he mostly chooses to play with. You may not want to include those children who will talk throughout the whole conversation. If another child is doing all the talking, there is no need for the quiet child to contribute. Give careful consideration to the membership of the group and to the time you hold the small-group conversation. Do not pull the child from one of his favorite learning experiences, for example, or hold the conversation in a noisy and distracting place. If transitions or change are unsettling for the child, do not hold conversations close to transition times between learning environments or different learning experiences.

Some children will feel more inclined and more comfortable talking to you while they are in the act of doing something such as building, drawing, or painting. Perhaps a child will talk more about a story you read with him while he's sitting snuggled up in a quiet spot on some cushions. The formal environment of a group conversation may be unfamiliar to the child. Perhaps his family does not operate in a conversational way, and the idea of an adult asking questions and listening to him is a strange and unnerving experience. He doesn't know what to do in conversation and doesn't understand what is expected of him. He may not yet have learned the natural rules of conversation or developed a sense of security about sharing his thoughts with an adult. It might take time for these to develop within the culture of conversation established in your learning environment. Your gentle, encouraging feedback and your belief in his abilities will support the quiet child to gradually feel safe to contribute.

Finally, for a child who is learning English as a second language, look for ways to provide conversational moments in his first language. Perhaps a family member can support you in this, or a community member who speaks the family language. Meet with them prior to their conversation with the child so you can explain your purpose. You might need a translator or interpreter for this meeting. Explain to them how you are interested to find out the child's ideas and thinking, not to test his knowledge. Explain how you would like the tone to be relaxed and to follow the child more than an adult just asking question after question. It would be helpful to ask the volunteer to watch you facilitate an informal conversation with a child in order to see your model: the tone you use, the body language, the gentle way of asking questions, and how you show interest in the child's ideas. It might be best to start this relationship in a specific way rather than saying to the volunteer "Just talk to them." Suggestions include reading a picture book or telling the story from the pictures in a child's first language, and then talking about the ideas in the book.

After the conversation, ask the volunteer to recall it briefly for you. Gain what insight you can from this, and don't worry too much if you don't get many "a-ha" moments. It is difficult to get inside a child's thinking when you are not the one in conversation with him. Remember that the experience of participating in a conversation in his first language will be a powerful learning experience, whether you are facilitating it or not. It is widely accepted that the stronger a child's first language, the stronger a second language will be. Through this conversation, he will have learned that his ideas are important to an adult, and that his first language is important at his early learning setting and to you. You can document the ideas shared by the volunteer, and give those ideas value by displaying them in the learning environment in both languages. A photograph of the child and adult, or the child's drawing of his ideas alongside his words in his first language and in English, gives powerful messages about the importance of all languages as a tool for thinking and learning.

Taking Ownership

How do you see the quiet child in your group? Reflect on your actions and words to him. Do they convey a belief in his ability as a learner, thinker, and participator in conversation? What are his strengths? How do you show you value these strengths in your program so that he becomes identified with and through them?

Track this child's participation in conversations for a week. Make a note in your planning book or journal each time he is invited into conversation. Be sure to note spontaneous as well as facilitated conversations. A chart such as the one in appendix B might help you.

At the end of the week, read through your documentation. What patterns do you see? Are there more opportunities for spontaneous conversations than facilitated? Does he seem more comfortable in one-to-one conversations than small-group conversations? Are you unconsciously valuing facilitated conversations over spontaneous conversations when reflecting on this child's participation? Does he participate more in spontaneous conversations? Is there a particular time, learning experience, or place in the room where he participates more freely in conversation?

Uncovering Children's Thinking

There are other ways to contribute to the thinking life of a learning group besides talking. The educators in Reggio Emilia talk of the hundred languages by which to understand the world and by which a child can express himself (Edwards, Gandini, and Forman 1998). If we think of language as "voice," then for the early childhood teacher, the young child has many voices that require our attentive listening. Sometimes we concentrate only on the kind of voices most valued by school culture and society: verbal and print communication. Without taking anything away from the importance of learning to communicate in the primary language of a community, children use other symbolic languages to express and communicate their thinking. It is these other voices that will help you listen with intent to the child with developing language.

The first key to listening with intent to children's other voices is becoming aware of them. Once you decide to value the learning and thinking that happens through languages such as art, construction, dramatic play, and movement, you can't help but notice more and more of what is happening during these moments. Reflect on what you currently give attention to. Are you spending a lot of time at the block area and very little time watching and listening to the learning and interactions at the painting easels? Do you regularly put out clay but rarely spend time watching what the children do with it? You can decide to have a different focus each week to help train yourself to value the learning taking place in the areas where you rarely spend time. For example, you might decide to focus on the drawing table for a week, and so make plans to spend five minutes of each choice time/ play time being in the moment with the children.

When children play and interact with materials, they create symbols to represent their ideas, their thinking, and their images of things. This is why they can be referred to as "symbolic languages." What do you pay attention to in the languages of clay, blocks, wire, or sand? How do you notice the thinking that happens there? Some ideas are:

- Use your eyes to watch rather than your ears to listen.
- Be in the moment just as you have practiced when listening to children's oral language.
- Take your time and don't rush your watching. Sometimes these languages take longer to reveal a child's thinking than oral language.

- Watch for movements, adjustments, and actions as the child interacts with the materials.
- Watch how the child uses a material to symbolize (or stand for) another object (for example, does the block symbolize a car along a road, or do Popsicle sticks symbolize trees in the sandpit forest?).
- Watch for problems a child encounters and ways he overcomes them.
- Watch the *process* of creating and using the language. Be interested in how the child creates from the beginning through each step along the way.
- Document the process by sketching, photographing, or videotaping.

We'll now look at examples of listening to the symbolic languages of imaginative play, block construction, and drawing.

Imaginative Play

Children's play offers great insight into their schema. Listening to the voice of a child while he plays will help you better understand the child's unique world, and can show you things not so clearly revealed through other voices. The child who is quiet or rarely participates in whole-class or small-group discussions might come into his own while playing.

When Nicholas was a little older than two, he needed to stay at a hospital for a fairly major operation. His big brother, four-year-old Daniel, watched from the sideline as his parents, with worried faces and serious words, prepared Nicholas for his hospital stay and for the scary events associated with doctors, medicine, injections, and going to sleep in a strange place. The whole family took Nicholas to the hospital and spent time with him in this new environment. Daniel's mother remained at the hospital with Nicholas so he would not have to stay alone. Daniel and his dad, Michael, returned home, and Michael set about preparing dinner for them while Daniel played in the next room. After a while, Michael called Daniel to dinner, and Daniel emerged wrapped in bandages with a stethoscope around his neck and his toy doctor's kit on his arm. "You need needle, Daddy," he announced, and proceeded to show Michael where he was hurt and how the bandages were helping him get better.

It must have felt strange to Daniel to come home to a quieter place with just him and his father. He might have been wondering when Nicholas and his mommy would come home again. In all the care and concern for Nicholas, no one had really thought much about the questions and confusions Daniel might have, but this didn't seem to matter because Daniel innately knew how to help himself feel safer and more at ease with these strange events. He knew he could play out the ideas in a safe and risk-free environment, and that his play would help him make some sense of it all. There was something about the experience of taking Nicholas to the hospital that Daniel could not express in words. It was too deep and perhaps too unknown for him to have the words to tell his father what he was thinking. Instead, play provided him with the voice he needed.

In your program, a child with developing language might be able to express his thinking more fully through imaginative play, just as Daniel did. He might not have the words to express his ideas or feelings, but his play might show you his schema and prior knowledge.

The quiet child in your program might feel more confident taking on a different role in imaginative play. Often children show greater self-confidence when playing a more powerful role in this secure environment. They get to try on the capabilities of another person: a mommy, a daddy, a firefighter, a superhero, or a magic fairy. The quiet child might feel safer talking and participating in this risk-free environment, which may reveal to you much more of his thinking than when he participates in conversations. Listening both to the language of talk during imaginative play and the language of the play itself will help you gain greater insight into the schema of young children.

Four-year-old Paolo shows us the power of listening to the language of imaginative play with a story from when he was in preschool. Paolo is Deaf, and at the time of this story his ASL was gradually developing. He understood more than he showed his teachers by his use of ASL. He played enthusiastically in the block area, would occasionally choose to paint or draw, and had recently discovered the dramatic play area of his classroom. However, he rarely took an active role in whole-class or small-group discussions, preferring instead to watch and listen, taking in as much of his new language as possible. His teachers saw a slowly emerging vocabulary in his language as he labeled items, and a developing ability to focus on conversations and understand turn-taking.

One day, the class inquiry topic was about the local pizzeria restaurant. As a group, the children had taken field trips to the restaurant, made pizza in class, and observed and drawn various ingredients and tools used in pizza making. Paolo's teachers wondered about his experience. What did Paolo understand from this exploration? What did he see or notice during the field trips? What was his schema about restaurants? About cooking? It was Paolo's play that offered insight to his teachers. His teachers watched his play more closely than usual and documented it by taking photographs throughout the playtime. Later they put the photographs together to provide a complete picture, and realized that within a fifteen-minute experience, Paolo's play revealed a rich schema about the pizzeria and cooking, including:

- an understanding of the role of the cook, pretending to prepare food near the oven of the class "restaurant"
- knowledge of the separate areas of a restaurant: his play remained in one area of the dramatic play area, and he did not venture into the area where the table and chairs were for customers
- knowledge of the process of preparing and baking a pizza: rolling the dough and placing it on the pizza tray, sprinkling toppings, placing it into the oven using the tray with the long handle, and waiting awhile before taking it out of the oven
- an understanding of the need to be careful when using the oven by using gloves to protect his hands
- knowledge of the uniform of the cook, as he chose to wear an apron and a chef's hat

Paolo's developing ASL could not reveal the depth of his understanding. However, the language of imaginative play not only gave him the avenue to continue constructing knowledge, it also offered his teachers a window into the private world of his thinking.

Now that his schema was at least partly revealed to them, they could explore possibilities of how to stretch Paolo's thinking. They could provide more opportunities to make small-group field trips, during which Paolo could more closely observe the cook at work. They could use this experience to guide Paolo's awareness of the relationship between cook and waiting staff. His teachers could also plan for experiences cooking and preparing a variety of food dishes, stretching Paolo's thinking from pizza to other kinds of food preparation techniques. Adding some cooking tools to the class restaurant might be a provocation for Paolo to use these in his play and reveal more of his knowledge and understanding. Finally, another possibility was to provide experiences to stretch Paolo's understanding of the different roles of the wait staff and customers in a restaurant. Having a small view into Paolo's existing schema, his teachers could now see how successful these new experiences would be in stretching his thinking.

Imaginative play does not occur only in the class dramatic play area, of course. The block area is another venue for imaginative play, as children create structures for a zoo, a Spider-Man city, or a castle for fairies, for example. Four-year-olds Christopher and Javier worked side by side in the blocks most days during class investigation time. They rarely chose to play in other dramatic play areas, and their work seemed to focus only on building and making, not on any imaginative thought. Their play was parallel rather than cooperative, but their ideas seemed to relate to each other as they built their structures side by side. As with the rest of the day, little conversation happened between the boys during their block play. While listening to their block play one day, their teacher noticed a new kind of structure being built by Christopher, and soon he was lying inside the long rectangular shape. Javier walked over to the home play area, and returned with a teddy bear to give to Christopher. The structure was a bed and the teddy bear was to help Christopher go to sleep! The documented block play revealed the boys' capacity for imaginative thinking that was not evident at other times. It revealed Christopher's imaginative world and his understanding of a shape that would enclose him as a bed. Most powerfully, the language of play showed Javier's capacity for empathy and thoughtfulness, plus his schema of what happens at bedtime (you cuddle with a teddy bear). Neither boys communicated these ideas with words, but their play let their teacher inside their thinking and provided a window by which to view the boys more fully.

Taking Ownership

Spend some time listening with intent to the ideas expressed in your dramatic play area or in another area where children are imagining in their play and interactions. You might choose to sit quietly to the side of the play area, or set up a video on a tripod. Document what you see happening rather than what you hear.

What is revealed to you? What do the children do with the play props and other materials? Does it show a connection to a real-world understanding or a real-world/adult use of materials? What does it show about the children's knowledge (schema) about using these materials in life?

What role is each child taking in their imaginative play? How do their actions show what role they are playing? How does their use of materials show you the role they are playing? What is the connection to real-world roles? What does it show the child knows about this role?

How do the children interact with each other? Does their play connect even if there are no words to connect it? Do they take particular roles? Are the roles related? What schema about relationships is revealed by their play?

Block Construction

Children's three-dimensional structures give voice to their emerging mathematical, physical, and social understandings. By building with blocks, young learners can experience the force of gravity when their constructions have difficulty standing, or indeed fall down (with or without applied force!). They can explore concepts of stability and balance while working through a process of trial and error to solve design problems. They learn about the characteristics of materials, such as size, shape, and texture, and develop their own categories for grouping materials. As they build, they also learn skills and strategies in design and construction. All this learning will be made visible by listening carefully to the language of block construction. Let's look at some examples to help explore this idea further.

Nancy noticed that the three-year-olds in her class seemed stuck in a pattern of building the same kind of low-lying structures with the blocks. The same group of boys would always choose to build, and they created long roads or tracks and flat buildings, often using the same kinds of blocks over and over again. Nancy wanted to stretch their ideas about the possibilities within the block area. She was surprised that the boys built only low-lying structures, given they lived in the middle of Manhattan with all its skyscrapers. She also hoped to entice a wider group of children to explore the possibilities of block construction.

This group of three-year-olds included children who were learning English as a second language as well as children with developing expressive-language abilities. Facilitating whole-class and small-group conversations about buildings with this group resulted in only one- or two-word responses from the children. So Nancy decided to take the children on a neighborhood walk. She hoped the focused observation and discussion about tall buildings, and the different shapes and various design features the children noticed, would expand the children's ideas about design, shape, and space. Nancy planned to document the children's block constructions by photographing them over the next few days. With her colleagues, she would use this documentation to interpret the children's thinking and look for any changes in their constructions that might reveal a stretch in their schema about buildings.

The day after the fifteen-minute neighborhood walk, Nancy was excited to see a change in the children's block constructions (see the photograph on the next page). For the first time that year, the children built upward. Their constructions seemed to communicate the closeness of the Manhattan buildings. While the buildings didn't touch, the space between them seemed smaller in response to their increased height. One child placed different-shaped blocks on the very top of her building, which the teachers hypothesized represented her observations of the different-shaped roofs or the water towers on the tops of buildings. The three-year-olds did not use their words to tell Nancy that their ideas sprung from the buildings they saw during the walk, nor did they tell her about their decision to build upward. The block constructions themselves spoke to her.

The skyscrapers built by three-year-olds after a neighborhood walk

The children's buildings that day revealed:

- a possible integration of new information into the children's existing schema about buildings: they built higher and used different-shaped blocks at the top
- an awareness of urban space in their buildings: the buildings were placed quite close to each other
- an awareness of high and relatively narrow buildings, representing their schema about skyscrapers in their view of Manhattan
- an awareness of how the different positioning of blocks creates different looks or can be for different purposes (one child turned a rectangle block to stand on its narrow base)

- an understanding of different surface features and their relationship to each other (one child's building showed a cylinder placed to stand on its flat base rather than on its curved surface)

By listening to the voice inherent in the children's block constructions, Nancy and her colleague Sam gained insights that helped them plan further ways to stretch the children's thinking. Possibilities included taking more neighborhood walks to photograph buildings, including some close-up shots of particular features of interest to the children. The photographs could be displayed on the surrounding walls or put in a binder in the block area so children could use them as reference for their own constructions.

Another idea was to give the children disposable cameras and ask them to photograph parts of buildings that were of interest to them. Nancy could also search for coffee-table and children's books about various building structures in order to add different images for the children's reference. Later on, when revisiting the documentation (photographs of the first skyscrapers), other possibilities emerged. The teachers noticed that most children were not including doorways (although they thought the rectangular block placed upright on the floor in one construction could possibly represent a door), so a topic on a future neighborhood walk could be the different types of doorways into buildings. And finally, a future possibility could be to explore elevators and stairs with the children by asking the provoking question: "How do the people get from the street to the top floor?" Many learning possibilities were revealed, in this case not from the children's words but by the meanings conveyed within their block constructions.

Four-year-old Petra belonged to another group of children. She was very quiet and reserved during class meetings, in small-group conversations, and even at mealtimes. Her teacher encouraged and invited her to participate, which she would do with short responses, but mostly she chose to be a listener. Petra's teacher wanted to find out more about Petra's interests and understandings, and so she decided to listen more closely to her play. Petra loved playing in the block area. She always played alone, and showed an ability to play for long periods of time and remain focused on a task she set herself. Photographs taken of Petra's block work showed her emerging mathematical knowledge and understanding. By looking closely at the end product of her castle with parking lot (shown in the photograph on the next page), a group of teachers interpreted the following:

- an awareness of lines in the shape of the castle and the line of cylinders on the left

- an awareness of shape, size, and symmetry in her choice of similar blocks to create turrets on top and the circles for car parking spots
- a keen eye for order shown in her sense of design, placing four circles at the end of four rectangles for the parking spots, matching the four turrets placed evenly along the top of the castle
- an understanding of matching lengths, in choosing a shorter rectangular block to go on top of two blocks on the left, as opposed to the longer rectangular blocks needed to match the length of four blocks in the middle and right of the castle structure
- an understanding of one-to-one correspondence in matching a car to each circle, a triangle to each turret

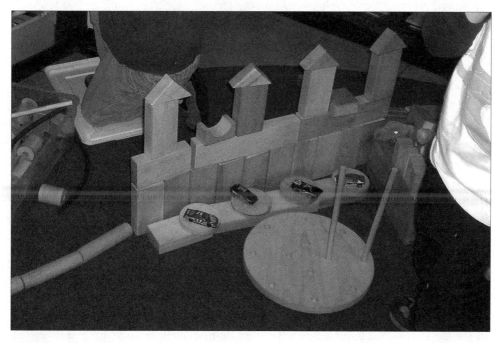

A castle with parking lot

It would be interesting to listen to Petra's other languages and observe other ways she might show her thinking, such as in her drawing or painting. Providing markers and paper on clipboards in the block area might serve as an invitation to draw a representation of her structure, therefore providing a new voice for the teacher to listen to. Providing different or unusually shaped materials as a provocation to her thinking about shape, size, line, and other characteristics is another possibility. Her schema about curved lines (as opposed to the straight lines she explored here) could be stretched by adding materials that hold this quality or by looking at photographs of structures that have curved features. This structure did not have an inside space. Perhaps asking, "How do the people get inside?" might provoke new ideas for Petra to use in her future design and construction.

The previous two examples show ways of interpreting the end product of a child's block construction work. Doing so highlights understanding and knowledge that are useful to the children's teachers, but it is only half the story. To fully appreciate the potential for uncovering children's ideas in block construction, teachers must also look carefully at the *process* of construction itself.

One day I decided to sit with three-year-old Davide while I was visiting his center. I visited here each week, but felt I hadn't yet connected with him. He was a reserved and quiet child who would most often choose to play alone. His family spoke Spanish at home, while the primary language of his preschool was English. However, when his teacher spoke to him in Spanish, he would respond with only one- or two-word answers. She was concerned about his language development, and felt she knew little about his understanding and development because he was so quiet and reserved. Davide loved puzzles, playing at the water table, and building with blocks.

The day of my visit, Davide chose to use the table blocks. I sat near him, but decided not to talk. I wanted him to feel comfortable with my presence and did not wish to force any interaction. I decided to practice being in the moment by watching and listening. I carried a clipboard with a blank copy of a documentation template (see appendix C).

As my documentation shows (see the photo on the next page), Davide chose two small blocks, a triangle, and a semicircle. The blocks were relatively the same size and thickness. First Davide placed the semicircle so it would stand on its curved edge. The block was thick enough to be stable. He then placed the triangle on top of the flat part of the semicircle, but because he placed the triangle with only half of the base on the semicircle top, it overbalanced, causing both blocks to fall to the left. When Davide picked up the triangle and tried a new strategy, I knew I was witnessing one of those extraordinary moments of learning that occur every day. Through a process of trial and error (more clearly displayed in the documentation), Davide explored the geometric properties of the blocks, discovering the semicircle's center of gravity. He then repeated the process with another set of identical table blocks, only this time he did not need to go through the same process of trial and error. He placed the triangle close to the semicircle's center of gravity from the start.

Date: 11/30/05	Children: Davide (3.4 ~~~~)
Observer: Lisa	

Context: At table during Choice Time, alone. Playing with small table blocks.

	Teacher Reflection
Moves blocks around table doesn't appear to have a set plan?	How do I know he didn't have a plan?
Uses 2 blocks △ ▽	
1. △▽ placed like this & they fell	
2. △▽ moved △ over to R slightly fell again	Power of an "ordinary moment" Wouldn't have become extraordinary if not for documentⁿ process!
3. ⊖ success!	
Repeated process with 2 other blocks same shapes. Started with △ in middle of ▽ and so only had to make slight adjustment to R to get balance	Transfers his learning to new context Practices & tests his theory?

Documentation of Davide's discovery of the center of gravity

Davide did not discuss his thinking aloud. Only by paying close attention to the *process* of Davide's block work was I able to witness his learning and the integration of new ideas into his existing schema.

Taking Ownership

Watch a quiet child next time he is in the block play area. Or ask him to play with you at a table with some open-ended materials. Decide how you will document the learning: scribing, photographs of the process, sketches, or video-taping? Listen with your eyes as much as your ears.

Find some quiet time later and ask a colleague to interpret this documentation with you. What do you see? What happened as this child interacted with the materials? Did his interactions give you clues to what he was thinking? What problems did he encounter and how did he solve them? What sense do you get about his disposition (or attitude) toward this kind of learning experience?

Drawing

Drawing is a language accessible to most children. I love how artist and educator Ursula Kolbe describes drawing as giving "wings to the imagination" (2005, 3). Drawing allows our imagination (our creative thinking) to fly. It also gives our thinking a voice. Just as words bring our thinking from the private to the public world, drawing makes our thinking visible. As Kolbe says, "Drawing can nurture children's abilities to think, feel and imagine, and to share ideas with others" (45).

Like the other voices we have explored, drawing can both reveal a child's ideas and provide the stimulus to stretch thinking. Sometimes children use drawing to express their thoughts or experiences, and at other times they use drawing to plan or create new ideas. When you listen carefully to the language of drawing, you have the chance to see what the child might not voice aloud. You have the chance to see some of the invisible, private world of the child's thinking. Drawing will not reveal a complete picture of a child's thinking, but learning to pay attention to it will give you a glimpse inside. A child's drawing can reveal:

- the artist's understandings or knowledge of the world
- how the artist solves problems with the composition or with the materials

- choices the artist makes
- movement (as opposed to representing objects)
- relationships between people or objects
- feelings or emotions
- a sense of story

There are two main reasons to use drawing for the purpose of listening to the ideas of young children: it provides a safe, comfortable environment and stimulus for conversation, and it gives voice to a child's unspoken thinking.

For the child who is quiet and reserved, drawing might provide an environment where he will feel comfortable to speak. A large-group conversation might be too confrontational for him, but sitting alongside his teacher while he draws might open the door for conversation to occur. The child must have a choice about what he is drawing, of course. A climate of security will not be achieved if you ask a child to draw something specific. Many children will talk about their drawing as they draw. They might label what they do, make plans for what they will do next, or chat about something that does not immediately appear connected to their drawing. You can encourage interaction and social learning by setting up materials and the environment to allow children to draw side by side or face-to-face. A table large enough for two to four children to reach materials and have enough space for their paper provides an environment rich with shared learning and conversational moments. At other times you can set up the drawing materials at the easels, which when placed alongside each other also encourages conversation.

One day, four-year-olds Cameron and Nula knelt on cushions side by side at a low table that their teacher had set with paper and markers. Both children were absorbed in their drawing. They were both quiet children in class, often seeming overwhelmed by the more rambunctious children in their group. The intimate setting of the small table, set in a quiet corner of the room, seemed to bind them together. Their teacher sat near them for a few minutes, watching their drawing closely. Cameron looked over at Nula's detailed drawing, and then glanced at his paper.

Cameron:	What that?
Nula:	Princess.
	[Cameron continues his drawing but seems unhappy with his attempts. After a few minutes more of drawing and scribbling, he speaks to Nula.]
Cameron:	Show me.
Nula:	What?

Cameron: That. Show me.

[Nula proceeds to show Cameron how she drew a princess. He watches intently, and then tries for himself.]

While this isn't an elaborate conversation, the intimate nature of drawing side by side bound Cameron and Nula together in a relationship. It gave them a purpose to be together, and ultimately a purpose for talking. This opportunity might have been lost if their teacher had not set the drawing table so thoughtfully, or had interrupted their drawing too soon with too many direct or leading questions. Sometimes just setting the environment or valuing it with your presence is enough to show children that a learning experience is important.

In another example, teacher Stacy set up a table for a drawing exploration of a pumpkin. She chose four children from her group of three-year-olds. One child's language was expressive and confident, and she was talkative in class. The three other children's expressive language was developing, and they were much quieter. She wanted to provide an experience in which the children could develop their vocabulary, and she chose the safe setting of drawing because the children were already experienced with drawing with black markers. It was a familiar setting using familiar materials.

Stacy began by facilitating a conversation about the pumpkin in the center of the drawing table. She asked the children open-ended questions such as What do you see? What do you notice? How does it feel? She also guided their observations and embedded new vocabulary within meaningful conversation by saying things such as "Can you see the line here? See how the line goes from the top of the stem to the bottom of the pumpkin." After exploring and talking, they drew the pumpkin both whole and cut apart. During the conversation and the drawing, the three quiet children began to use new words they learned from Stacy and from their more verbal classmate. Stacy noticed two children used the new words "pumpkin" and "bumpy," and another used the new words "heavy" and "squishy" when talking about the pumpkin. The exploration and the experience of drawing the pumpkin gave them a reason to be together and to talk with each other. The drawing part was important to continue the children's learning: it was not just an add-on to the end of the facilitated conversation. During the following circle time, Stacy asked these children to share their drawings and experience with the rest of the group. This gave them another opportunity and reason to use language. Their drawings connected them to the experience, and they had a more intimate knowledge of pumpkins through the process of drawing. The drawings were displayed with pride in the classroom, which provided another opportunity for the children to revisit their learning and use their new words when they showed their families later in the week.

The second reason for using drawing, to give voice to a child's unspoken thinking, is a strategy that will help you listen to children with developing language. In the same way that the voices of block construction and imaginative play reveal a child's thinking, drawing can provide a glimpse inside a child's inner world.

It is easier to interpret a drawing when a child uses words to explain or describe it to us. It gives us clues as to what various sections of the drawing may represent. You can interpret drawings without the accompanying language, but you must be cautious of making assumptions about a child's thinking based only on how one drawing looks.

It is important to remember not all drawings will directly represent things in the way we might picture them. It might not show us a clear image or likeness to the object, person, or idea the child talks about. "Mommy" might not look at all like a person. A "car" might not have wheels. This does not mean a child has no concept of people or of wheels on a car. As with expressive language, children know a lot more than they are able to draw.

It is also important to remember that the meanings children attach to their drawings might change. They might change in the process of drawing. What starts out as a cat can change to a plane (particularly if one flies overhead while the child is drawing!). A drawing about home can become a drawing about the park, evolving somehow during the child's creative process. It might also change over time, transforming its identity from one day to the next.

Drawing will often add to your understanding of a child's thinking in ways that his oral language might not. A child with developing language might not have the vocabulary (that is, he might not know the words) to express his ideas. Remember, just because he doesn't talk about something doesn't mean he doesn't have an understanding of it. Drawing can sometimes show you what his words cannot.

In chapter 6, we met Jordi while he was involved in a facilitated conversation about thinking. Jordi is developing competency in two languages: his home language of ASL, and English. At the age of five, both of his languages are considered developing, and have been labeled as delayed. During the facilitated conversation (in which I needed to use his second language of English), Jordi told me that the brain does the thinking. He also told me that the brain is in your head. At times I had trouble understanding Jordi's English, so I asked if he would draw what his thinking looked like (see the photo on the next page).

The meaning I interpreted from Jordi's drawing added to my understanding of the ideas he expressed in English words:

- Jordi drew a whole person with the brain drawn inside the person's head. Drawing a whole person could show his understanding of the connectedness between the brain, thinking, and a whole person. The brain is not separate from the person as a whole. Perhaps this is his way of showing the brain influences what the whole person does.

- He drew the brain with a face, and then added the head around the brain, drawing another face for the person's head. This puzzled me at first. Then I remembered the other children at the drawing table talked about how the brain "tells us what to do." Jordi drew his understanding of this by giving the brain a face with a mouth and eyes. It is like his drawing is saying, "If the brain talks to us, it must have a mouth and eyes because that's how we talk to each other." Jordi used his schema of "talking" to make sense of how the brain would communicate to the person.

- Jordi then drew circular marks swirling inside the brain. Often the lines children draw do not represent an object, nor are they meaningless "scribbles"; lines can represent movement or some other phenomena not easily communicated in a static medium. Jordi's circular lines may represent the working of the brain, the thinking that is happening. It shows he understands that thinking is an active process, not a static event or an object. The lines could be interpreted to represent the synapses making connections within the brain. Although Jordi does not have the vocabulary to express this, nor a sophisticated understanding of brain research at his disposal, he can use the language of drawing to communicate his ideas about the true essence of thinking.

Jordi's drawing of the brain thinking

Taking Ownership

How can the voice of drawing be louder in your learning environment? How can you listen to the children's drawing more? Start by collecting drawings for a week or so. With a colleague, spend time looking at and interpreting them. What do they tell you? Refer to the list earlier in this chapter on pages 164–65 to help you with your interpretation.

Conclusion

When teachers listen with intent to children, they hear beyond the words and listen to their thinking and to their ideas. This is easy with some children because they are verbal and expressive, talkative and gregarious. Other children ask more from teachers. They call teachers to search for other ways to hear beyond their words and listen to their ideas. By listening to their other voices, such as their play, block construction, and drawing, you can gain a glimpse into the private world of their thinking. It may take time for these other voices to reveal a child's schema, but the rewards are large when you connect to children's thinking and gain a much richer perspective of them as learners.

References

Edwards, C., L. Gandini, and G. Forman, eds. 1998. *The Hundred Languages of Children.* Greenwich, Conn.: Ablex Publishing.

Kolbe, U. 2005. *It's Not a Bird Yet: The Drama of Drawing.* Byron Bay, New South Wales: Peppinot Press.

CHAPTER EIGHT

Using Conversations Purposefully

Documenting children's conversations is a means to an end, not an end in itself. Interpreting your documentation will reveal possibilities for stretching the children's schema about the world. Not using the documentation you collect is like a half-baked cake—only half the potential is realized. This chapter will explore ways to make the best use of the conversations you capture in your documentation by using your insights into the children's schema to plan a rich and engaging curriculum for them.

After working with your colleagues to interpret your documented conversations and construct an understanding of the children's ideas, how do you decide what to do with this information? The first thing to do is decide what your original purpose was for capturing the conversation. This purpose will be closely linked to your intended audience for the documentation. While not exhaustive, I see three main purposes for most documentation, each of which will be explored in this chapter:

1. to guide curriculum planning—the audience is primarily teachers (you and your immediate teaching colleagues)
2. to share with children in order to develop reflection and self-direction in learning—the audience is primarily the children
3. to communicate about learning with families and the wider community—the audience is other adults (families, colleagues, and community members)

The same piece of documentation can serve all three purposes and be shared with all audiences, but it is not always necessary to do so. For example, teachers Vanessa and Dawn videotaped the imaginative play of their kindergartners over the course of a few weeks. They videotaped twice a week for about ten minutes at a time. The main purpose for this documentation was to interpret the children's use of language form (in ASL, English, and play) in order to research possible connections between story time and children's authentic language use. Vanessa, Dawn, and I viewed the videos together, interpreting and hypothesizing about them. We made plans from them (although we always had more ideas than we could realistically implement) and wondered aloud about the children's thinking.

These videos could also have been shared with families or shown to the children, but in this case, the documentation served its purpose in guiding the planning of curriculum, and was left at that.

Guiding Curriculum

The process of capturing conversations, interpreting them, and using the documentation is a dynamic cycle. Our initial interpretations illuminate children's thinking and show us a glimpse of their schema about an idea or topic. Perhaps we discover some emerging theories they have about the world, ways in which young learners use their prior knowledge to make sense of ideas that are puzzling or complex to them. Now that we have some knowledge of their understanding, we can plan ways to stretch these ideas by playing, drawing, creating, building, reading, listening, and talking. The conversations give teachers starting places for curriculum planning.

Let's say you have collected conversations, and with your colleagues have interpreted meaning from them. During this interpretation process you would have looked for ideas in the children's words that could spark further exploration and thinking, such as the children's:

- questions ("How does the elevator know when to stop?")
- confusions, misunderstandings, or emerging theories (Teacher asks, "Where does milk come from?" Child responds, "In carton. My mommy buys it at the store.")
- analogies or metaphors ("The lights are dancing," or "My brain is like a balloon.")
- interest or excitement ("Look! Look! Snail over here!")
- unusual views ("The leaves are friends together on the tree.")

- observations ("I can see a rainbow in the glass!" or "The princess lives in the tower here.")
- ideas ("Rain in clouds, come down.")

Now you are ready to design a curriculum that can explore these ideas further and provide ways to stretch the children's schema. Planning for experiences that will stretch young learner's thinking often involves creating the conditions for intellectual conflict we explored in chapter 1. This conflict might arise naturally as two children talk about their emerging theories and discover differing ideas, or you might challenge or stretch their ideas by offering a particular question or alternative view during a facilitated conversation. At other times, materials will offer the opportunity to stretch children's thinking. Materials, questions, and firsthand experiences become, as Reggio Emilia educators call it, a provocation to children's thinking (Edwards, Gandini, and Forman 1998). The following experiences offer opportunities for provocations to children's schema, ideas to talk about during your conversations, and a meaningful context for learning new vocabulary:

- field trips
- visiting experts and artifacts
- observational drawing
- firsthand exploration with materials
- facilitated conversations

Field Trips

Field trips offer many opportunities for firsthand experience and, therefore, opportunities for children to research their ideas. However, we too often limit the value of field trips by planning them at the end of a unit or as an end-of-the-year excursion. Somehow our idea of field trips is stuck in a view of something a little frivolous, a fun add-on or a concluding experience. A different idea of field trips sees them as a necessary and integral part of curriculum design, where young learners are able to experience for themselves aspects of life that stretch their schema and understandings (Harris Helm and Katz 2001).

When interpreting a conversation, look for possibilities for field trips. Ask yourself these questions:

- Do the children's ideas connect to a real-world place?

  For example, the ideas children express while cooking and eating in imaginative play connect to the real-world places of restaurants, kitchens, cafeterias, and supermarkets. The ideas children express when talking about their new boots for jumping in puddles connect to the real-world places of a shoe store, a shoe factory, and of course, a park or playground where there are lots of puddles after it rains.

- Do the children's ideas connect to a real-world job, role, or activity?

  For example, the ideas children express when they talk about electric fences on their block castles connect to the job of an electrician. Children who talk about a new baby brother or sister express ideas that can connect to the role of parent, midwife, nurse, or doctor.

- Where might children see this idea in action?

  For example, the ideas expressed by children when talking about shadows connect to a field trip to the playground at a particular time of the day, where there is space and a large wall to watch their shadows more closely. Children who talk about a windy day as they arrive in the morning express ideas that can connect to a field trip to a park on a windy day, armed with ribbons on poles to watch the wind move, or to a park when there are many autumn leaves on the ground, so they can watch how the wind blows them around.

- Is there an "everyday" place nearby to visit that connects to the ideas children are talking about, rather than exploring the idea only within the walls of your building?

  For example, can you visit the neighborhood diner or laundry to explore ideas about cooking and eating or washing clothes, which children talk about during their imaginative play? When children talk about numbers while they count the cars on the trains they build, their ideas connect to a neighborhood walk to look at different house numbers. When they talk about shapes as they create patterns on the light table, their ideas can be extended by a walk to explore mailbox shapes or different-colored doors on the street. Imagine how many more conversations would be sparked from these field trips.

There is also great value in return visits to the same site, an idea that has not been traditionally embraced in early learning settings. How many times have you heard teachers say, "But the children went there last year?" This thinking can limit possibilities for learning and truly deepening understanding. Think about adult research for a moment: If you are learning about a new idea, researching about something of importance or relevance to your teaching or to your leisure, do you refer to only one text? Whether I want to deepen my understanding about pedagogy, traveling to Peru, or renovating my home, I refer to more than one text, and I also find myself returning to the same texts many times. These revisits help me make more connections between the ideas in the text and the ideas in my own thinking.

Field trips can offer a similar experience for young learners. The first visit to a site may be exciting and overwhelming, or even a little scary for some. Children will most often take in a generalized view during their first visit, eagerly taking in as much as possible but not spending much time observing or thinking about one particular idea or area. Some learners will be overwhelmed by such a new experience, their anxiety impacting their impressions and thinking about the visit. By returning to the same site, we give young learners the opportunity to look more closely at particular features or characteristics. You can use return visits to a site to follow up on particular interests that children showed during the initial field trip, therefore providing an experience that can help deepen their ideas and stretch their schema.

Let's look at these examples to help us more clearly connect young learners' words with field trips that could stretch their experience and ideas about the world.

On a neighborhood walk, this conversation was documented:

Eden: I found a church because church got red doors. And they have yellow candles inside.

Sebastian: This is a circle with leaves on it and a circle inside it—over the doors of the church [referring to the stained glass window].

Eden: It's a big window for the church to look outside.

What possibilities for field trips emerge from the ideas expressed in this conversation? The children's interest in the stained glass windows of the local church to suggest further neighborhood walks to study churches and their windows would extend their experience and internal ideas. Do all churches have red doors? Do all churches have stained glass windows? How do we know it is a church if it doesn't have these things? What do the windows look like from the inside? What different shapes and colors are used in stained glass windows?

As this inquiry progressed, the following morning-meeting conversation was documented by Marilla, one of the children's teachers:

Ellen (teacher): What do you see out of a window?

Zara:	Rooftop and you can open and close.
Polly:	School.
Timmy:	Flag.
Rory:	You could see trees and branches and windows and churches.
Anna:	I'm just going to say trees.
Tabor:	When you look out the window you can see fire trucks.
Andrew:	Glass.
Sebastian:	Cars.
Zeke:	Glass and the window.
Rory:	What's glass?
Anna:	It's used to make things and it's something that you could break.
Rory:	If you touch on the point you can get hurt.

A possible question to challenge these young children to stretch their thinking would be "What do you see out of different windows?" or "What is the view from different windows?" A way to explore this with them would be a field trip to take in the views from different windows. The experience of this field trip could be used to spark further conversations. You could take the children to look through windows on different floors of the school building, or through different windows in your home. What is the view from windows at the front, side, and back of your building? Field trips can happen right in your own learning environment.

Taking Ownership

Reread some of the conversations you have recently documented. What field trips could stretch the children's ideas about the things they talk about? Will you take the whole group or a small group of interested learners? How will you capture the experience to bring back to your learning environment?

Visiting Experts and Artifacts

While preferable, it is not always possible to arrange multiple field trips for the purpose of children's learning. Perhaps the site is not particularly open or welcoming to this way of working with young children, and one visit is all you can arrange. Perhaps there isn't a suitable site close by where you can easily and regularly take small groups of children. In these situations, you can explore ways to bring the resource to your early learning setting rather than the children to the resource. Two ways to do this are through the use of experts and artifacts. When listening closely to the children, listen for ideas that connect to real-world jobs and real-world items. Here you will find possibilities for experts and artifacts. You can then:

- Invite an expert to visit your program.
- Ask an expert to bring an artifact with her to show and talk with the children about.
- Ask an expert to lend you an artifact.
- Use everyday artifacts in deeper study with children.

EXPERTS

For example, there may be one person from a field-trip site who would be interested in developing a longer-term relationship with the children. Can you invite this person to meet with children in your setting? The openness and confidence of the visiting expert in working with young learners will influence what is possible. Taking time to help prepare the expert will pay off once she is interacting with the children. You can:

- Meet with the expert before the visit, or at least talk on the telephone or via e-mail.

   Person to person is always preferable, of course. This means you will also feel connected to the expert, and it will be a more rewarding experience for you: it won't be just welcoming a stranger into your program, because you will know each other.

- Ask children what their questions or interests are before the visit.

   This prepares them for the visit and gives you information to share with the expert. Very young children might have difficulty giving you questions. The concept of a question is still developing in their minds. Be alert to what they find interesting and to the spontaneous questions they ask as they interact and play. What was it that alerted you to invite this expert in the first place?

- Talk to the expert about the interests and questions of the children so she is prepared to talk with young children.

Tell the expert why you contacted her. What was the initial conversation that sparked this idea?

- Take or send a copy of the children's conversations that are connected to the expert's role.

  This will help her get in touch with the children's interests and also connect to them as thinkers and people, rather than just "three-year-olds." She will even know some of the children's names before she arrives.

- Compose a letter to the expert with a small group of children.

  Use the children's language and ideas. Tell the expert what sparked the children's interest and what they want to find out more about. Add a photograph of the writers so the expert feels connected to them.

There are different ways to structure the expert's visit. It does not always need to be the visitor talking to the whole group or just answering the children's questions. Other ideas include:

- Ask the visiting expert to be part of a learning experience rather than just talking to the whole group.

  Being part of a small-group experience can connect the visiting adult and the children through a common experience. It provides a firsthand experience for the children to learn from and learn through, and a rich environment for spontaneous conversation. For example, a tailor could help the children measure each other with tape measures, a worker from a garden store could plant quick-growing beans or sunflowers with a small group, a painter could help the children mix colors, or a grandmother originally from Mexico could make fresh tortillas with a small group.

- Ask the expert to bring an artifact from her work or hobby to show and talk about.

  This is particularly helpful when talking with young children because it will focus the children's attention. It also helps the visiting expert. Many adults are not accustomed to talking with young children, and having an object to talk about can help them feel comfortable. For example, a builder might bring her tool belt, or a chef might bring the tools he uses to make pasta. When teachers Dave and Peggy and their kindergartners worked on an inquiry project about service dogs, they invited a dog groomer to visit the class. She brought grooming tools with her, and showed how she used each tool properly. This provided a much richer conversational experience both for children and adults than the question-answer interview format so often used with visiting experts. Other examples include: a doctor can bring a medical bag or first aid kit, a potter can bring a potter's wheel or different types of clay, and a builder can bring blueprints or brick-laying tools.

ARTIFACTS

If visiting experts are unavailable to visit the learning environment, all is not lost. While the human source of information offers a rich and dynamic conversational moment, specific artifacts or objects also bring possibilities for learning and conversation. Perhaps the visiting expert is only able to make one visit, but the experience and conversation can be extended long after the visit through the use of artifacts the visitor left for the children to explore. Similarly, when you can't find an expert willing or able to come to your learning environment, consider what artifacts or objects you could bring into the learning environment for children's exploration. For example, you may not be able to arrange for a visit from an architect, but you can obtain plans and designs for young learners to use while working in the block area. It may not be possible for a veterinarian to visit, but you can introduce a pet such as a fish or an ant farm and establish an area for children's ongoing observation and conversation. In the absence of a mechanic, a set of real-life tools could spark children's curiosity and imagination in discovering how they are used and what their purpose is.

If teachers see children as competent and capable, then they need to trust them with materials that may not traditionally be considered child-friendly (and they should teach the children how to use and care for them properly). For example, during an inquiry project about buildings with her three-year-olds, Nancy introduced the artifacts of a hammer, a screwdriver, and a spirit level. She took time to show the tools to the children and to talk about their uses and safety aspects. They were placed at the drawing table for the children to explore more closely, and they were free to move them and touch them as they needed. Nancy then introduced one or two tools into the block area for the children to play with. She always ensured there was supervision nearby so she felt secure in her duty of care for the children. She reinforced the proper way to use these tools, just like the builders they saw during their field trip, and like Brady's dad, who visited and showed the children his tool belt. Nancy was thrilled to see the children treat the tools with respect and care as they used them in real-life, appropriate ways while building their block constructions.

Some materials might be too fragile or precious to let children use independently. If children are not able to actively use and play with the materials, they still have value in stretching children's ideas. They can be displayed in an interesting and appealing way so as to ignite children's curiosity and engage them in conversation. Teachers and children gathered around a new or unusual object can talk about its features, imagine its uses, and even talk about ideas for making a replica they can play with. The object is like a surprise for children's minds and imaginations.

In another example, when the children in Marilla and Ellen's class were fascinated by the different musical instruments used in *Peter and the Wolf*, the school music teacher, Dan, was invited to visit with the children each week. He brought a different musical instrument each time, and showed the children how to play each one, how to create different sounds, and how to clean and care for them. With Dan's guidance and encouragement, the children were invited to hold and play each instrument. He then generously left the instrument in the room for a week, during which time the children could touch, play, draw, and study it up close. This firsthand experience led to greater understanding and appreciation of music.

Let's look at an example inspired by children's ideas in the following conversation. Ellen and Marilla often introduce an unusual object for the children to wonder and talk about. This particular day the mystery object was a collapsible rubber funnel:

Eddie:	I think it's for the bath so the water can come here. It would get on somebody's body.
James:	When I hold it like this . . . look what happens! But this has to be longer. Maybe it needs one of these here so it could make a scratching noise. [he opens and closes the object]
	It's an air machine!
Adam:	Sadie, James, and me think it's a machine that gives you cold air when it's hot.
Sadie:	It's a hat for a leprechaun.
Karl:	A hat because it was a hat because it could bend and everything the hat can do and the hat can stay on the mirror and it could fall.
James:	When it goes up it gets big with a magnifying glass.
Eddie:	A birthday hat.

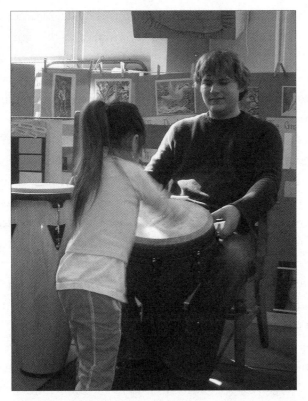

Visiting expert Dan involves children in firsthand experience with musical instruments.

Artifacts for the dance inquiry project

What are some ways to stretch the ideas of these young learners? A selection of different styles of hats could be placed near a mirror so children could try them on and see what they look like. Imagine the authentic conversation that could flow from this experience. The hats could also be placed at the drawing table, or you could take photographs of the children wearing different hats and then invite children to draw their portraits wearing the hats.

James's and Adam's comments about machines are intriguing. What might their schema about machines be? You could ask the boys to draw what the "machine that gives you cold air" looks like and show how it works. They could be challenged to make the cold-air machine with found materials or clay. You could ask the provoking question "What other machines give you cold air when it's hot? How do they work?" and facilitate further conversation, drawing, or construction.

Sometimes introducing new artifacts is an appropriate way to stretch children's ideas and experiences. For example, these children could look at machines in their learning environment (such as the overhead projector, the CD player, or an old typewriter) and this would help their teachers discover more about their schema about machines. Simple machines that might be in the children's homes such as pasta-making machines, mixers, and washing machines offer further exploration possibilities. Locating an old machine that could be taken apart so the children could look inside would be a fantastic artifact to stretch their schema and invite more conversation. It could lead to drawing, constructing, playing, and lots of talking.

Observational Drawing

Sometimes referred to as drawing "from life," observational drawing is a tool for thinking that can be used to stretch children's schema. It's connected to providing artifacts—you need something to draw, after all. Observational drawing encourages children to learn to notice details, to observe closely, and to be curious about the world. These are essential skills for learning for life. Observational drawing helps children communicate what they see and what they think, through their words and through their drawings. It also binds children in conversation when two or more children are invited to draw the same object, to see the same object through their own eyes, and therefore have the opportunity to talk about their observations and experience.

When documenting and interpreting conversations, listen for the same clues that suggest providing a real-life artifact to stretch the children's schema (see previous section). If the artifact has interesting lines, shapes, or other features, it could be an interesting object for the children to get to know better through drawing.

Observational drawing can become a valuable research tool for you and the children. When listening closely to their ideas in their conversations, listen for moments that children could express through drawing. When you discover an artifact that would stretch children's schema, use it for conversation and drawing. By drawing the artifact, children build a more intimate relationship with the object. The two become friends as they interact through the drawing process. Some tips for successful observational drawing include:

- Choose artifacts to draw that have interesting but simple lines and shapes.

  When starting observational drawing with young children, choose objects with simple lines and interesting features. A ball has simple lines but no interesting features that will make it interesting to draw. A child could draw this in a few seconds. A pumpkin has simple lines, like the ball, but also has interesting features in the lines and different colorations along the skin and the stem. As the children become more familiar with drawing, you can present more complex shapes and lines to them.

- Arrange the drawing table to show its importance.

  Place the artifact at the center of the table on a black cloth or a slightly raised stand. A cake stand might work well for some objects. This sets it apart from everything else in your room and shows that it is important. Arrange the drawing table with a sheet of paper and a marker for each child, like a place setting. This communicates clearly what you expect to happen at this area.

- Spend time looking closely and talking about the artifact before drawing.

  Don't just put the artifact out on the table and say, "Draw it." Guide the children to discover all the lines, shapes, bumps, smooth parts, colors, and features of the object. Let them touch it, smell it, and look at it from different perspectives. Can't you just hear the rich conversation during this experience?

Observational drawing as part of a service–dog inquiry

Observational drawing outdoors—a study of trees

Three-year-old Marco drew a self-portrait one day and told his teacher Nancy, "My mouth is mad. I'm mad. Imogen made me mad because she is playing over there. My nose and cheeks. My cheeks are red."

Indeed, his self-portrait showed those red cheeks. How can Nancy use Marco's ideas as a catalyst to explore further through observational drawing? You could introduce an artifact such as a mirror or photographs of faces showing different feelings to stretch his ideas about his emotions. Placing the mirror on the drawing table, with paper and markers nearby, would be an invitation for Marco to study his features more closely. It would be interesting to watch how this influences his drawings and conversation. To challenge his thinking even further, an interested adult could sit with him as he observes himself in the mirror, asking him what his face looks like when he is feeling different emotions: "What does your face look like when you are happy?" "Show me what your face looks like when you are scared." You could also take photographs of Marco and other interested children showing different emotions on their faces, and then laminate the photos or place them in frames to become inspiration for children's observational drawing and quality conversation.

Taking Ownership

Reread some recent conversations you have documented. What possibilities for observational drawing emerge from the children's ideas? Are there certain artifacts associated with the topic of their conversation that could become inspiration for observational drawing? Will drawing certain ideas help young learners explain their thinking or make their schema more clear to you?

Firsthand Exploration with Materials

In chapter 5 we discussed open-ended and closed questions, and how open-ended questions support young learners to talk more widely about their ideas. The kinds of materials you provide for children to learn with and learn from can also be either open-ended or closed. Open-ended materials can be used in more than one way; closed materials have only one right way to be used or one right solution. For example, here's a list of some open-ended and closed materials commonly found in early childhood learning environments. Perhaps you can add more to the lists.

OPEN-ENDED MATERIALS	CLOSED MATERIALS
blocks	jigsaw puzzles
assorted collage materials	craft templates
paper, markers, crayons, pencils	coloring books
fabric in assorted lengths, colors, and textures	role-defined dress-up clothes

Open-ended materials offer more possibilities for exploring, problem solving, negotiating, designing, creating, and discovering than materials that have only one way to be used. Open-ended materials are like those "fat" questions, full of potential and abundant with opportunities for conversation. Closed materials are like "skinny" questions: their possibilities are limited.

I'm not suggesting you should have no closed materials for children to use. Sometimes closed materials, such as jigsaw and floor puzzles, offer important learning challenges. It is more helpful to think of the choice between open-ended and closed materials not as either/or. Rather, think in terms of more open-ended materials and fewer closed materials.

Adding new and interesting materials to your learning areas can provide challenges to the thinking of young learners. Teachers Peggy and Dave made a trip to a store that specializes in reused or surplus materials from factories and other businesses, and bought a selection of door knobs, cardboard cylinders, and corrugated cardboard. These materials were added to the block area and became inspiration for many creative constructions, including the snowflake factory we read about in chapter 1. Teachers Kathie, Carol, and Ferdinand added restaurant-themed play props to their dramatic play area. The apron, notepad, pencil, menus, and cash register acted as provocations for the children's understandings of social interactions, vocabulary, roles, money, print literacy, and restaurant-language discourse, and the children explored their emerging understandings through their play. Teachers Ellen and Marilla visited the hardware store and bought lengths of plastic tubing and funnels for children to design and create their own musical instruments. Adding materials with different properties, such as plastic tubing (which has the ability to bend), or natural materials like shells or pinecones to the block or dramatic play area creates new ideas and new reasons for children to talk.

What can you look for in children's conversations that might be a spark to add open-ended materials to their play and exploration? Ask yourself these questions:

- Does the conversation show a connection to adult work or activity?

  For example, a conversation about the nearby construction site and getting the bricks to the top floors connects to the real work of using pulleys and levers. You could add pulleys and levers to your block area. This would provide open-ended possibilities for children's exploration, conversation, and learning.

- Does the conversation show an interest in particular roles for imaginative play?

  For example, if children were talking about going to the doctor's office, you could add open-ended materials that could be used to extend the play and conversation of these roles. Adding pieces of white fabric to the imaginative play area would allow children to use them for hats, aprons, slings, and so on.

- Does the conversation show an interest that you want to extend?

  For example, if you notice conversation and play about trains, you might add open-ended materials like tubes or half cylinders that can be tunnels and bridges in block play.

Let's look at an example with four-year-olds William, Carlos, and Tran as they are playing at a light table in Jason, Kathie, and Ferdinand's room one day. Kathie documented their words:

William:	Hey, look! My pocket card is getting dark on the light table.
Carlos:	[puts his name card on the light table] Oh, yeah. Look at this.
Tran:	[places his name card on top of Carlos's] Put this one on top and it's dark!

This conversation sparked a long-term inquiry into dark and light, which in turn evolved into exploring shadows. When we reread this documentation later we imagined other possibilities for stretching the boys' learning about the properties of materials through their light-table play. A collection of different materials could be placed on the light table for the boys to discover which ones let light through and which ones "went dark." Questioning could guide them to make generalizations about the properties of materials. What kinds of materials let the light shine through? What are they made of? Are the materials that "go dark" made of the same kinds of things? What kinds of materials in the room do you think would let the light shine through? What groups of materials can you make? Young children can be guided to collect items from their learning environments and to use their emerging theories to make predictions about each item's ability to let the light shine through. They could be asked to share their discoveries with the rest of their learning group at a meeting time. New possibilities for explorations and new theories about the properties of materials could emerge from all the diverse ideas talked about by different learners.

Sometimes your decisions about adding open-ended materials will not be sparked by particular ideas you hear in your documented conversations. Rather, you may decide to introduce new open-ended materials to children because of the lack of ideas you hear in their conversations. For example, children who have played together at the table blocks for months might not have a lot to talk about. Adding new and interesting materials, such as rope, clear tubing, or colored beads, could challenge them to do new things with their building. The new materials offer endless opportunities for exploring, problem solving, and, of course, for conversation, as children learn how these new materials interact with the ones they are already familiar with.

Taking Ownership

Look around your learning environment. How many open-ended materials do you provide for the children to explore and discover with? Can you add some new and interesting materials? Remember, you might need to remove and store some of your existing materials so your learning environment doesn't become too cluttered.

Facilitated Conversations

Sometimes sharing transcripts happens incidentally or spontaneously, like when a child asks you to read to her what you have written. At other times you will want to reintroduce a transcribed conversation in a more planned way during a facilitated conversation. An idea from an initial conversation can help reconnect young learners to the ideas and also spark new conversations that explore and stretch their schema more deeply. Let's look at a story from Rose's preschool group to explore how you could do this.

Kenia, Jessie, Leon, and Garrett were playing in the block area, working industriously to build a castle. Teacher Rose sat to the side of the block area, not involved in the play, scribing the conversation.

Kenia:	Watch the circle so it can't fall.
Garrett:	We need electricity walls. This is outside.
Kenia:	Where's the door?
Garrett:	We don't want the bad guys to get in!
Kenia:	Here, we'll put a special door that's full of potatoes.
Garrett:	No, I have an idea. We'll put this high so they can't get in.
Kenia:	And they'll have to jump over! Much better.
Jessie:	We need a roof.
Kenia:	Yes, we do.
Gavin:	I'll put it on.
Kenia:	I will too because I'm the builder.
Garrett:	Me too.
Kenia:	Oh, it fell, look what you did!
Garrett:	Let's just build it again.

Rose and I met soon afterward, and during our interpretation of this conversation, we were struck by the part where Garrett talks about the electricity walls outside. We became very curious about his understanding of electricity, and documented our questions in our meeting notes.

- Why does he think we need electricity outside?
- Is it connected to his prior knowledge of street lights? For protection from the bad guys? Stop signs?
- Does Garrett associate electricity more with outside than inside?
- What does he think electricity is?
- How are the bad guys and electricity connected in his thinking? Are they connected for him, or is it our inference that connects them?
- How can we find out what Garrett thinks about electricity?

We decided to explore it further. Rose planned for a facilitated conversation with Garrett and Leon, as they had been playing together in the block area consistently for the last week. We brainstormed some possible questions Rose could ask during the conversation. This helped prepare her thinking and language, and she kept this list close by but didn't use it as a script. These questions are not in any particular order, but reflect our brainstorm of possibilities:

- What were you thinking about when you were playing that day?
- What do you know about electricity?
- Why did you need electricity?
- What will the electricity do to the wall?
- How does it work?
- Where do we see electricity outside?
- Where is electricity?
- What do we need electricity for?
- How do we use it?
- Is there electricity inside too? What does it do?

Rose began the facilitated conversation by reading aloud the initial scribed conversation (it had not been typed but remained as Rose's scribed notes and served its purpose in this form). She showed the boys a photograph of the castle they worked together to build that day. We hoped this would help reconnect the boys with the experience, and particularly Garrett with his thinking about the electricity wall. We were very conscious that a few days had passed and wondered whether we were asking too much for Garrett to reconnect to an experience and to his thinking days earlier.

"When you built the castle, you said this—I'm going to read it to you now because I wrote down just what you said." Rose proceeded to read aloud from the transcribed conversation, ensuring that she read it as a whole first, and then reminded Garrett of what he said about electricity. "We need electricity walls. This is outside." Rose waited for thinking time and leaned forward to show her interest in the children's ideas.

Rose:	Where do we see electricity outside?
Garrett:	I never saw electricity, but I did play Operation and saw electricity. Metal on metal. It's light blue. It's kind of cracky.
Rose:	So why would you need it for your castle?
Garrett:	You could use it for lights. There's electricity in wires.
Rose:	Oh, where does it go?
Garrett:	It comes out in the light. I think I know what's happening to our light [that is broken]. It's not getting enough electricity. Electricity comes from plants. They use gloves I think to get the electricity out. The sun for a light, but it doesn't need electricity.
Rose:	What lights up the sun then?
Garrett:	I don't know.

Leon:	Sometimes cords light up the sun and cords have electricity. When you break it electricity comes out.
Rose:	Where does it come from?
Leon:	[points to the wall] Right there.

From the documentation of the facilitated conversation with Garrett and Leon, Rose and I could see many possibilities for exploring the boys' ideas further. We thought about possible field trips, visiting experts, artifacts, play materials, and drawing experiences that would provide a provocation or an invitation to the boys. These included:

- Ask Leon to draw his ideas of the sun being lit by cords.
- Explore the workings of electricity in lights by studying and drawing lamps, spotlights, and other lighting in the classroom.
- Can the school custodian show the children the inside wiring of a lamp or other inside workings of electrical machinery?
- Add wire (from the hardware store) to the block area and observe how children use it to show their ideas about electricity.
- Ask Garrett more about how he connects electricity and plants. Share the conversation with his family and see if their knowledge of Garrett's prior experience may reveal a connection he is making. Perhaps he could draw his ideas and show us how "they" get the electricity from the plants?
- Explore the sun as a light further by reading books about the sun and listening further to the children's ideas about it.

As frequently happens, we discovered more possibilities than were possible to implement, but the process of thinking without limits can bring greater creativity to your planning. The idea of wire in the block area sparked our curiosity, and we decided to follow this road as a next step. We also decided if the children continued to show interest in and curiosity about the idea of electricity in wire and cords, Rose would talk with the custodian about other possibilities for a small-group exploration.

Sharing with Children

Displaying children's words alongside their artwork and photographs of them engaged in the learning process surrounds children with the idea that their words and thinking are important. When teachers share their documented conversations with children it helps them:

- See and hear their words more clearly

  Hearing their words aloud through another's voice can help children hear their ideas more clearly. When a teacher reads a transcript aloud to a child, she hears her words in an adult voice, and this gives them some importance in her eyes. It is like a mirror. The reflection of a mirror can allow us to see ourselves more clearly. The reflected words from the teacher's voice allows the child to hear her ideas more clearly too.

- Revisit the learning experience and their ideas

  Children will often ask adults to read the displayed transcripts to them, almost as if they want to revisit the experience, like a dear friend you want to visit again and again. Each time they reconnect with their learning experience there is an opportunity to deepen or stretch learning.

- See the value of their words to organize their thinking

  The very act of writing down a child's words communicates their importance. As Zaphira, teacher of three-year-olds, says, "Sometimes when we have a class discussion, I'll be the one writing down what they say in a notebook. Quite often, the children will come over afterward and say, 'Where's *my* name? What did *I* say?' It creates a sense of delight when they see their words written down just as they said them."

  When a teacher reads a child's words aloud, the child has an opportunity to see how important they are to organize her thinking. When the child's teacher uses her words to start conversation or lead to another experience, the message the child gets is, "It is important to talk about our ideas because it helps us learn." Talking about thinking is valued by the teacher, and so the child learns that it is an important thing to do.

- Be reminded of and therefore reconnect to an idea or experience

  We earlier discussed the value of being a memory tool for young children. When you want to reconnect a child or small group to an experience, reading a transcript of their conversation is a great way to draw them in. Remember how well this strategy worked for Rose when she read her transcript of the electricity conversation to the children?

Children ask Marilla to read documentation to them.

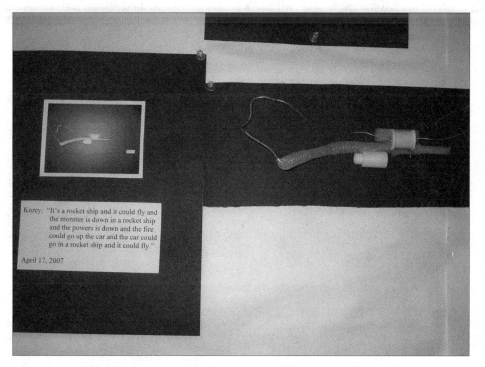

Korey: "It's a rocket ship and it could fly and the monster is down in a rocket ship and the powers is down and the fire could go up the car and the car could go in a rocket ship and it could fly."

April 17, 2007

Children's words make their thinking visible.

Communicating with Families

The benefits of building positive relationships with young children's families are well documented. Children have been shown to be more successful in their schooling when their families are involved in their schooling. Sharing documentation with families is a strong strategy for building such relationships. It will help:

- families feel connected to what is happening at your early learning setting
- children see that their families think their learning is important
- families trust you, because they will see you know their child and are interested in her
- families see the everyday learning of their child; they will value this everyday learning assessment rather than focusing only on checklist assessments for their understanding of their child
- you work with families toward the same learning goals for their child
- you know the children better, because you will know their families through your conversations with them about the documentation

Let's look at an example that shows how teachers Jason and Rose shared their documentation with children's families. The teachers had collected documentation in the form of photographs and children's language and wished to use it to communicate important ideas about learning to the families. Their purpose and their audience were clear. Due to the long distances the children traveled to school (they traveled by schoolbus from all five New York City boroughs), they decided that sending newsletters home was the most effective form of communication, since parents rarely had the opportunity to be at the school. During planning meetings, they discussed shifting the emphasis of the newsletters from generalized sharing of events to more focused sharing of the learning and thinking of the three- and four-year-olds. To communicate this effectively, they decided to focus each newsletter on one question or idea that existing documentation could highlight for families, or on a question or idea that the teachers were interested in collecting documentation about and therefore researching themselves. Here is their initial list of possible questions they could use as the focus of the newsletters:

- Do young children cooperate with each other without the insistence of an adult?
- Can children teach each other?
- How do children explore length and height?
- What are our children curious about?

- How does drawing help children show us their thinking?
- What do children learn through block play?
- What decisions do children make each day?
- How do children take responsibility at school?

Jason and Rose decided to use a guiding question for each newsletter, and then selected specific photographs and samples of children's language they felt best communicated their ideas (see appendix E).

Many early childhood educators now produce a portfolio for each child as a way to share the richness of the learning process with families. You can easily add a transcribed conversation into a child's portfolio, and in fact including it will be an important way to show families the value you place on children's words and thinking. Keep the following points in mind when preparing a transcribed conversation for a child's portfolio:

- Provide some context for the documentation.

  The audience (the family) will not necessarily know the context of the conversation you have selected. Write a brief statement telling the reader where the conversation took place or if it was connected to a larger inquiry project. You could also add a photograph of the group of children involved in the conversation as a powerful way to place the reader in the learning context with their child.

- Briefly interpret the conversation.

  Write a brief interpretation of the child's ideas expressed in this conversation. Do not overwhelm the family with every possible interpretation. While this depth of thinking is helpful to you as an educator, put yourself in the shoes of the child's family and think about what they would be most interested in or the main idea that is important to communicate to them. You can show you value a child's language and thinking with an interpretation consisting of two or three carefully crafted sentences.

- Use accessible language.

  Think carefully about the language you use when writing about the context or the interpretation of the learning. Do not use teacher jargon, which can overwhelm some families and at the very least be difficult for non-educators to understand. Is the family non-English-speaking? If this is the case, you will need to have the context statement and the interpretation translated into their home language. Perhaps there is another parent or community member who can help you with this. Many communities offer support services for this important translation work, so you may find the help you need by looking online or by asking the family for advice on who to contact.

- When appropriate, use samples rather than the entire transcript.

  A family does not need to read a complete conversation. Including just a phrase or a sentence will show the family how much you value children's words and how you can gain important insight into their thinking by listening carefully to them. You might include a phrase lifted from a larger conversation, or perhaps a child's conversation about a painting, block construction, or favorite book. The important thing is to make the child's words a highlight of the portfolio, not just the teacher's words. See appendix D for an example of a conversation prepared for a child's portfolio.

These steps for preparing documentation to share with families will also help you prepare for other ways of sharing. You can display documented conversations with a context statement and photographs or with children's drawings in your learning environment. Rather than place them on walls and leave it to chance, ask families to read and talk with you about the displayed conversation. You might say something like "Have you seen what Rory said about the chrysalis and butterflies the other day?" and together explore the words displayed. Remember, some families might speak languages other than English or might not have written-English literacy proficiencies. Displaying documented conversations and inviting families to look at the displays with you will provide the opportunity for you to read the conversation to them in a nonjudgmental and purposeful way. Similarly, you can use documented transcripts of a child's conversation during family-school conferences or parent-teacher meetings.

Conclusion

At the core of *Are You Listening?* is the belief that each child is filled with the potential for learning and thinking, and is capable and competent. Children's ideas show intelligence and logic as they make new connections and build emerging theories about how the world works. Conversations offer a window into this thinking, where we can view a child's private world—a world of promise, curiosity, and beauty. This view also helps us better design and implement curriculum that is relevant, meaningful, and responsive to children's schema. Curriculum that provides ways to stretch children's ideas and allows them to construct new understandings about the world. Curriculum that is designed with the child in mind. In these days of back-to-basics activism and the likelihood that high-stakes testing will be extended into the early childhood years, it is also essential to advocate for the kind of early childhood environments where children's ideas are valued.

Relationships are at the heart of quality learning and teaching. The teacher's role is critical in establishing open, respectful, and warm relationships with children and with their families. Conversation is a powerful tool for building relationships, and the ideas and strategies shared within these pages are offered as a way to support you in this essential work. In order to build relationships, we must be willing to risk a little of ourselves when we reach out to others first. When we commit to listening to children and to their families before pushing our own agendas, we build many bridges between the child's two worlds of home and school. For this kind of listening we need to listen with our ears, our eyes, our minds, and our hearts. In doing so, we show the next generation the power of listening and of understanding others. Can we dare to dream that this is our contribution to building a future filled with hope and understanding? I hope so.

References

Edwards, C., L. Gandini, and G. Forman, eds. 1998. *The Hundred Languages of Children*. Greenwich, Conn.: Ablex Publishing.

Harris Helm, J., and L. Katz. 2001. *Young Investigators: The Project Approach in the Early Years*. New York: Teachers College Press.

APPENDIX A

Interpreting the Teacher's Role:
Categories of Teacher Interactions

INTERPRETING THE TEACHER'S ROLE
CATEGORIES OF TEACHER INTERACTIONS

Date:	Participants:
Context:	
Facilitated conversation:	

Supports child to join in play, learning experience, or conversation	
Supports child to problem solve	
Clarifies teacher understanding of child's idea or thinking	
Affirms or encourages child's efforts/ thinking/work	
Wonders aloud (models questioning)	
Models curiosity	

Stretches child's thinking (challenges or provokes)	
Seeks information about the immediate (for example, asks to retell, to describe or to label parts of child's work if drawing or blocks)	
Delves deeper into children's ideas	
Connects to prior experience, or is a memory for the child	
Gives the child an adult solution to a problem	
Leads child toward the teacher's idea	
Brings conversation back to the topic	
Other	

APPENDIX B

Tracking Children's Participation:
Participation in Conversations

TRACKING CHILDREN'S PARTICIPATION

PARTICIPATION IN CONVERSATIONS

Child:

Teacher:

Date	Time	Place	Topic of Conversation	F (facilitated) S (spontaneous)

APPENDIX C

Documenting and Interpreting Conversations

DOCUMENTING AND INTERPRETING CONVERSATIONS

Date:	Documented by:

Context:

Interpreted by:

Conversation Transcript	Interpretation

Possible next steps:

APPENDIX D

Sample Portfolio Page

SAMPLE PORTFOLIO PAGE

Name: Gregory	Age: 4.3 years	Date: 1/8/07

Context: Gregory and Vince have chosen to work in the block area during work time.

They left the meeting area and have just pulled a few assorted blocks from the shelves onto the block area rug. Vaisha enters the area.

Conversation:

Vince: I'll tell you what I want to do. I want to put all of these up.

Vaisha: Do you want to make a castle for the rabbit?

Vince: Okay. And I'm making a forest too.

Gregory: We'll need a door.

Vince: And a bed for rabbit. Maybe this [shows a cylinder].

Gregory: I have an idea for the bed. Does this work?

[puts a square block on a flat plank]

Vince: Yeah. Now we need spikes on the castle.

Learning:

This conversation shows Gregory's developing skills in negotiating his play. He no longer takes over the direction of the block play as he did earlier this year. His words show how he has learned to ask the other players for their ideas too.

This conversation also shows how he brings his prior knowledge to his play. He understands some of the essential characteristics of a building. It's interesting his first thought was to build a door. I wonder what he was thinking about? Maybe because the class rabbit is real to him, he was wondering how the rabbit will get inside the castle? It was like he had a clear picture of the rabbit inside the castle in his mind and used this as a tool to help him plan his play.

APPENDIX E

Sample Newsletter

SAMPLE NEWSLETTER

Pre-K

107

PS 347
ASL and English Lower School
225 East 23rd St., NY, NY 10010

November 2nd
Newsletter
Vol. 3

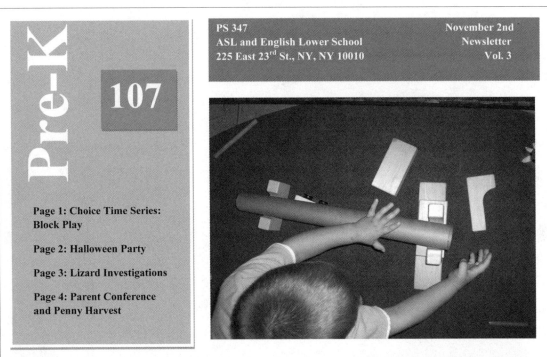

What do children learn when they play with blocks?

The conversation on the right was documented during Choice Time one morning. In this very short conversation we can see how much learning takes place when children are given the opportunity to make choices, to play freely with each other, and to use quality materials.

- Decision making ("We need more triangles")
- Problem solving ("Oh, we need a missing door")
- Knowledge of buildings (roof, door, people live inside)
- Knowledge of shape (triangles), length (matching blocks when building), symmetry (even-sided buildings)
- Spatial awareness (inside and outside space)
- Imagination and visualization
- Cooperation and team work
- Printed materials communicate messages (for example, a sign that says "Please don't touch.")

K: Oh, it stands up very good.

J: The people fell over. They did!

K: Uh oh, we need more triangles.

J: Why?

K: For the roof.

K: Jess, I need help so I can get my building fixed. Jessica, look! I'm making a stage for the peoples.

J: I see more grapes (half of clear plastic sphere). I need a little more sticks for the cake.

K: I need the top of the house, so the peoples can go inside the building. Oh, we need a missing door.